उत्तराध्ययन सूत्र

The

Uttarādhyayana Sūtra

Translated from Prākṛt

by

Hermann Jacobi

KSHETRA BOOKS
IDEAS EMBODIED.
www.kshetrabooks.com

The Uttarādhyayana Sūtra,
from the Jaina Sutras
(Sacred Books of the East vol. 45), 1884

Re-print of 1st Edition, 2015
with updated Sanskrit and Prākṛt transliteration.

Cover Design by Jon W. Fergus
Cover Photography, "Palitana Temples," by Pratap Tur.
Source: https://commons.wikimedia.org/wiki/File:Palitana_temples.jpg

ISBN: 978-1515192145

Contents

Introduction

About the work translated in this volume, the Uttarādhyayana, I have little to add to the remarks of Professor Weber in the Indische Studien, vol. xvi, p. 259 ff., and vol. xvii, p. 43 ff. The Uttarādhyayana, the first Mūlasūtra, belongs to the last section of the Siddhānta. Its intention is to instruct a young monk in his principal duties, to commend an ascetic life by precepts and examples, to warn him against the dangers in his spiritual career, and to give some theoretical information. The heretical doctrines [as found in works such as the Sūtrakṛtāṅga] are only occasionally alluded to, not fully discussed; apparently the dangers expected from that quarter grew less in the same measure as time advanced and the institutions of the sect were more firmly established. Of more importance to a young monk seems to have been an accurate knowledge of animate and inanimate things, as a rather long treatise on this subject has been added at the end of the book.

Though there is an apparent plan in the selection and arrangement of the single Lectures, still it is open to doubt whether they were all composed by one author, or only selected from the traditional literature, written or oral, which among the Jainas, as everywhere else, must have preceded the formation of a canon. I am inclined to adopt the latter alternative, because there is a greater variety of treatment and style in the different parts than seems compatible with the supposition of one author, and because a similar origin must be assumed for many works of the present canon.

At what time the works under discussion were composed or brought into their present shape is a problem which cannot be satisfactorily solved. As, however, the reader of the present volume will naturally expect the translator to give expression to his personal conviction on this point, I give my opinion with all reserve, *viz.* that most parts, tracts, or treatises of which the canonical books consist, are old; that the redaction of the Angās took place at an early period (tradition places it under Bhadrabāhu); that the other works of the Siddhānta were collected in course of time, probably in the first centuries before our era, and that additions or alterations may have been made in the canonical works till the time of their first edition under Devardhigaṇin (980 AV. = 454 A.D.)

I have based my translation of the Uttarādhyayana on the text adopted by the oldest commentators I could consult. This text differs little from that of the MSS. and the printed editions. I had prepared a text of my own from some MSS. at my disposal, and this has served to check the printed text.

The Calcutta edition of the Uttarādhyayana (Saṃvat 1936 = 1879 A.D.) contains, besides a Guzeratī gloss, the Sūtradīpikā of Lakṣmīvallabha, pupil of Lakṣmīkīrtigaṇin of the Kharatara Gaccha. Older than this commentary is the Tīkā of Dēvēndra, which I have made my principal guide. It was composed in Saṃvat 1179 or 1123 A.D., and is confessedly an abstract from Śāntyāchārya's Vṛtti, which I have not used. But I have had at my disposal an illuminated old MS. of the Avachūri, belonging to the Strassburg University Library. This work is apparently an abstract from the Vṛtti of Śāntyāchārya, as in a great many passages it almost verbally agrees with Dēvēndra's work.

H. JACOBI.

BONN, November, 1894.

Additional Note.

I may here add a remark on the Parable of the Three Merchants [see the seventh lecture], which agrees with Matthew 15:14 and Luke 14:11. It seems, however, to have had a still greater resemblance to the version of the parable in The Gospel according to the Hebrews, as will appear from the following passage from Eusebius' Theophania (ed. Migne's Patrologia Graeca, iv. 155), translated by Nicholson:

> "The Gospel according to the Hebrews (London, 1879): The Gospel, which comes to us in Hebrew characters, has directed the threat not against the hider, but against the abandoned liver. For it has included three servants, one which devoured the substance with harlots and flute-women, one which multiplied, and one which hid the talent: one was accepted, one only blamed, and one ṣut up in prison."

I owe this quotation to my colleague Arnold Meyer.

Taking into consideration (1) that the Jaina version contains only the essential elements of the parable, which in the Gospels are developed into a full story; and (2) that it is expressly stated in the Uttarādhyayana, Lecture Seven, 15 that "this parable is taken from common life," I think it probable that the Parable of the Three Merchants was invented in India, and not in Palestine.

H. J.

Translation

First Lecture: On Discipline

I shall explain in due order the discipline of a houseless monk, who has got rid of all worldly ties. Listen to me. (1)

A monk who, on receiving an order[1] from his superior,[2] walks up to him, watching his nods and motions, is called well-behaved. (2)

But a monk who, on receiving an order from his superior, does not walk up to him, being insubordinate and inattentive, is called ill-behaved. (3)

As a bitch with sore ears is driven away everywhere, thus a bad, insubordinate, and talkative (pupil) is turned out. (4)

As a pig leaves a trough filled with grain to feed on faeces, so a brute (of a man) turns away from virtue, and takes to evil ways. (5)

Hearing a man thus compared to a dog and a pig, he who desires his own welfare, should adhere to good conduct. (6)

Therefore be eager for discipline, that you may acquire righteousness; a son of the wise,[3] who desires liberation,[4] will not be turned away from anywhere. (7)

One should always be meek, and not be talkative in the presence of the wise; one should acquire valuable knowledge, and avoid what is worthless. (8)

When reprimanded a wise man should not be angry, but he should be of a forbearing mood; he should not associate, laugh, and play with mean men. (9)

He should do nothing mean,[5] nor talk much; but after having learned his lesson, he should meditate by himself. (10)

If he by chance does anything mean, he should never deny it, but if he has done it, he should say: "I have done it"; if he has not done it, "I have not done it." (11)

He should not, in every case, wait for the express command (of the teacher) like an unbroken horse for the whip (of the rider), but like a broken horse which sees the whip (of the rider) he should commit no evil act. (12)

Disobedient, rough speaking, ill-behaved pupils will exasperate even a gentle teacher; but those will soon win even a hot-tempered teacher who humour him and are polite. (13)

He should not speak unasked, and asked he should not tell a lie; he should not give way to his anger, and bear with indifference pleasant and unpleasant occurrences. (14)

Subdue your Self, for the Self is difficult to subdue; if your Self is subdued, you will be happy in this world and in the next. (15)

Better it is that I should subdue my Self by self-control and penance, than be subdued by others with fetters and corporal punishment. (16)

He should never do anything disagreeable to the wise,[6] neither in words nor deeds, neither openly nor secretly. (17)

He should not (sit) by the side of the teacher, nor before him, nor behind him; he should not touch (the teacher's) thigh with his own, nor answer his call from the couch. (18)

A well-behaved monk should not sit on his hams,[7] nor cross his arms,[8] nor stretch out his legs, nor stand (too) close to his teacher. (19)

If spoken to by the superior, he should never remain silent, but should consider it as a favour; asking for his command,[9] he should always politely approach his teacher. (20)

If the teacher speaks little or much, he should never grow impatient; but an intelligent pupil should rise from his seat and answer (the teacher's) call modestly and attentively. (21)

He should never ask a question when sitting on his stool or his bed, but rising from his seat[10] and coming near, he should ask him with folded hands. (22)

When a pupil who observes the above rules of conduct, questions the teacher about the sacred text, its meaning, or both, he should deliver it according to tradition. (23)

A monk should avoid untruth, nor should he speak positively (about future things, his plans, etc.); he should avoid sinful speech, and always keep free from deceit. (24)

He should not tell anything sinful or meaningless[11] or hurtful, neither for his own sake nor for anybody else's, nor without such a motive. (25).

In barbers' shops[12] or houses, on the ground separating two houses, or on the highway a single monk should not stand with a single woman, nor should he converse with her. (26)

Any instruction the wise ones[13] may give me in a kind or a rough way, I shall devotedly accept, thinking that it is for my benefit. (27)

(The teacher's) instruction, his manner of giving it, and his blaming evil acts are considered blissful by the intelligent, but hateful by the bad monk. (28)

Wise, fearless monks consider even a rough instruction as a benefit, but the fools hate it, though it produces patience and purity of mind. (29)

He should occupy a low, firm seat, which does not rock; seldom rising and never without a cause, he should sit motionless. (30)

At the right time a monk should sally forth, and he should return at the right time; avoiding to do anything out of time, he should do what is appropriate for each period of the day. (31)

A monk should not approach (dining people) sitting in a row, but should collect alms that are freely given; having begged according to the sanctioned rules, he should eat a moderate portion at the proper time. (32)

A monk should wait (for his alms) alone, not too far from other monks, nor too near them, but so that he is not seen by another party; another monk should not pass him to get the start of him. (33)

Neither boldly erect nor humbly bowing down, standing neither too close by nor too far off, a monk should accept permitted[14] food that was prepared for somebody else.[15] (34)

In a place that is covered above and sheltered on all sides, where there are no living beings nor seeds, a monk should eat in company, restrained and undressed. (35)

A monk should avoid as unallowed such food as is well dressed, or well cooked, or well cut, or such in which is much seasoning, or which is very rich, or very much flavoured, or much sweetened.[16] (36)

(The teacher) takes delight in instructing a clever (pupil), just as the rider (in managing) a well-broken horse; but he tires to instruct a foolish (pupil), just as the rider (tires to manage) an unbroken horse. (37)

(A bad pupil thinks:) "I get but knocks and boxes on the ear, hard words and blows"; and he believes a teacher who instructs him well, to be a malevolent man. (38)

A good pupil has the best opinion (of his teacher), thinking that he treats him like his son or brother or a near relation;[17] but a malevolent pupil imagines himself treated like a slave. (39)

He should not provoke his teacher's anger, nor should he himself grow angry; he should not offend the teacher nor irritate him by proclaiming his faults.[18] (40)

Perceiving the teacher's anger one should pacify him by kindness, appease him with folded hands, and promise not to do wrong again. (41)

He who adopts the conduct which the wise ones[19] have attained by their virtues and always practised, will not incur blame. (42)

Guessing the teacher's thoughts and the purport of his words, one should express one's assent, and execute (what he desires to be done). (43)

An excellent pupil needs no express directions, or he is (at least) quickly directed; he always carries out his duties as he is told. (44)

An intelligent man who has learned (the sacred texts) takes his duties upon himself,[20] and he becomes renowned in the world; as the earth is the dwelling of all beings, so he will be a dwelling of all duties. (45)

When the worthy teachers, who are thoroughly enlightened and from early times well versed in conduct,[21] are satisfied (with a pupil), they will make over to him their extensive and weighty[22] knowledge of the sacred texts. (46)

His knowledge will be honoured, his doubts will be removed, he will gladden the heart of his teacher by his good acts; kept in safety by the performance of austerities and by meditation, being as it were a great light, he will keep the five vows. (47)

Honoured by gods, Gandharvas, and men, he will, on leaving this body which consists of dirt and impurities, become either an eternal Siddha,[23] or a god of great power and small imperfections. (48)

Thus I say.[24]

Second Lecture: On Troubles [1]

O long-lived (Jambūsvāmin)! I (Sudharman) have heard the following Discourse[2] from the Venerable (Mahāvīra):

Here,[3] forsooth, the Venerable Ascetic Mahāvīra of the Kāśyapa Gōtra has declared twenty-two troubles which a monk must learn and know, bear and conquer, in order not to be vanquished by them when he lives the life of a wandering mendicant.

These, then, are the twenty-two troubles declared by the Venerable Ascetic Mahāvīra, which a monk must learn and know, bear and conquer, in order not to be vanquished by them when he lives the life of a wandering mendicant:

1. digañchā (jugupsā)-parīsahā, hunger;
2. pivāsā (pipāsā)-p., thirst;
3. sīya (śīta)-p., cold;
4. usiṇa (uṣṇa)-p., heat;
5. daṃsamasaya (daṃsamaśaka)-p., gad-flies, and gnats;[4]
6. achēla-p., nakedness;[5]
7. arati-p., to be discontented with the objects of control.
8. itthī (strī)-p., women;
9. chariyā (charyā)-p., erratic life;
10. nisīhiyā (naiṣēdhikī)-p., place for study;
11. sejjā (śayyā)-p., lodging;
12. akkōsa (ākrōśa)-p., abuse;
13. vaha (vadha)-p., corporal punishment;
14. jāyaṇā (yāchanā)-p., to ask for something;

15. alābha-p., to be refused;

16. rōga-p., illness;

17. taṇa-phāsa (tṛṇasparśa), pricking of grass;

18. jalla-p., dirt;

19. sakkārapurakkāra (satkārapuraḥkāra)-p., kind and respectful treatment;

20. pannā (prajñā)-p., understanding;

21. annāṇa (ajñāna)-p., ignorance;

22. sammatta (samyaktva)-p., righteousness.

[6]The enumeration of the troubles has been delivered by the Kāśyapa,[7] I shall explain them to you in due order. Listen to me. (1)

1. Though his body be weakened by hunger, a monk who is strong (in self-control) and does penance, should not cut or cause another to cut (anything to be eaten), nor cook it or cause another to cook it. (2)

Though emaciated like the joint of a crow's (leg) and covered with a network of veins, he should know the permitted measure of food and drink, and wander about with a cheerful mind. (3)

2. Though overcome by thirst, he should drink no cold water, restrained by shame and aversion (from forbidden things); he should try to get distilled[8] water. (4)

Wandering about on deserted ways, in pain, thirsty, with dry throat, and distressed, he should bear this trouble (of thirst). (5)

3. If a restrained, austere ascetic occasionally suffers from cold on his wanderings, he should not walk beyond the (prescribed) time, remembering the teaching of the Jina. (6)

"I have no shelter and nothing to cover my skin, therefore I shall make a fire to warm myself"; such a thought should not be entertained by a monk. (7)

4. If he suffers from the heat of hot things, or from the heat of his body, or from the heat of summer, he should not lament the loss of comfort. (8)

A wise man, suffering from heat, should not long for a bath, or pour water over his body, or fan himself. (9)

5. Suffering from insects a great sage remains undisturbed. As an elephant at the head of the battle kills the enemy, so does a hero (in

self-control conquer the internal foe). (10)

He should not scare away (insects), nor keep them off, nor be in the least provoked to passion by them. Tolerate living beings, do not kill them, though they eat your flesh and blood. (11)

6. "My clothes being torn, I shall (soon) go naked," or "I shall get a new suit"; such thoughts should not be entertained by a monk. (12)

At one time he will have no clothes, at another he will have some; knowing this to be a salutary rule, a wise (monk) should not complain about it. (13)

7. A houseless and poor monk who wanders from village to village may become tired of ascetic life: he should bear this trouble. (14)

A sage should turn away from this discontent; he should wander about free from sins, guarded in himself, a tabernacle (as it were) of the Law, doing no actions, and perfectly passionless. (15)

8. In this world men have a natural liking for women; he who knows (and renounces) them, will easily perform his duties as a Śramaṇa. (16)

A wise man who knows that women are a slough, as it were, will get no harm from them, but will wander about searching for the Self. (17)

9. Alone, living on allowed food,[9] he should wander about, bearing all troubles, in a village or a town or a market-place or a capital. (18)

Different (from other men) a monk should wander about, he should acquire no property; but not being attached to householders, he should live without a fixed residence. (19)

10. In a burial-place, or a deserted house, or below a tree he should sit down, alone, without moving, and he should not drive away any one. (20)

Sitting there he should brave all dangers; when seized with fear, he should not rise and go to some other place. (21)

11. A monk who does penance and is strong (in self-control), will not be affected beyond measure by good or bad lodgings, but an evil-minded monk will. (22)

Having obtained a good or bad lodging in an empty house,[10] he should stay there thinking: "What does it matter for one night?" (23)

12. If a layman abuses a monk, he should not grow angry against him; because he would be like a child,[11] a monk should not grow angry. (24)

If a monk hears bad words, cruel and rankling ones, he should silently overlook them, and not take them to heart. (25)

13. A monk should not be angry if beaten, nor should he therefore entertain sinful thoughts; knowing patience to be the highest good, a monk should meditate on the Law. (26)

If somebody strikes a restrained, resigned Śramaṇa somewhere, he should think: "I have not lost my life." (27)

14. It will always cause difficulties to a houseless monk to get everything by begging, and nothing without begging. (28)

The hand (of the giver) is not always kindly stretched out to a monk when he is on his begging tour; but he should not think that it would be better to live as a householder. (29)

15. He should beg food from the householder when his dinner is ready; a wise man should not care whether he gets alms or not. (30)

"I get nothing to-day, perhaps I shall get something to-morrow"; a monk who thinks thus, will not be grieved by his want of success. (31)

16. If any misfortune[12] happens and he suffers pain, he should cheerfully steady his mind, and bear the ills that attack him. (32)

He should not long for medical treatment, but he should continue to search for the welfare of his soul; thus he will be a true Śramaṇa by neither acting himself nor causing others to act. (33)

17. When a naked, rough, restrained ascetic lies on the grass, his body will be hurt. (34)

In the sun his pain will grow insupportable; still a monk, though hurt by the grass, will not use clothes.[13] (35)

18. When by the heat of summer his body sweats and is covered with dirt and dust, a wise monk should not lament his loss of comfort. (36)

He should bear (all this), waiting for the destruction of his Karman,[14] (and practising) the noble, excellent Law; he should carry the filth on his body till he expires. (37)

19. It may be that a gentleman salutes a monk, or rises from his seat on his approach, or invites him (to accept alms in his house): a monk should evince no predilection for men of this sort, who show him such marks of respect. (38)

Not resentful, having few wants, begging from strangers, and not being dainty, a wise man should not long for pleasant things, nor be sorry afterwards (for not having got them). (39)

20. "Forsooth, in bygone times I have done actions productive of ignorance, for I do not remember them when asked by anybody anywhere."[15] (40)

"Afterwards, however, actions productive of ignorance take effect." Therefore comfort yourself, knowing the consequences of actions. (41)

21. "It was of no use to turn away from the lust of the senses and to live restrainedly, for I do not properly recognise good and bad things." (42)

"Though in practising austerities and religious observances I live according to strict rules, still the hindrances to knowledge will not go off." (43)

22. A monk should not think: "There is, indeed, no life to come, nor an exalted state to be acquired by penances; in short, I have been deceived." (44)

A monk should not think: "Those lied who said that there were, are, and will be Jinas." (45)

All these troubles have been declared by the Kāśyapa. A monk should not be vanquished by them, when attacked by any anywhere.

Thus I say.

Third Lecture: The Four Requisites

Four things of paramount value are difficult to obtain here by a living being: human birth, instruction in the Law, belief in it, and energy in self-control. (1)

I. The universe is peopled by manifold creatures, who are, in this Saṃsāra, born in different families and castes for having done various actions. (2)

Sometimes they go to the world of the gods, sometimes to the hells, sometimes they become Asuras in accordance with their actions. (3)

Sometimes they become Kṣatriyas, or Chaṇḍālas and Bukkasas, or worms and moths, or (insects called) Kunthu[1] and ants. (4)

Thus living beings of sinful actions, who are born again and again in ever-recurring births, are not disgusted with the Saṃsāra, but they are like warriors (never tired of the battle of life). (5)

Living beings bewildered through the influence of their actions, distressed and suffering pains, undergo misery in non-human births. (6)

But by the cessation of Karman, perchance, living beings will reach in due time a pure state and be born as men. (7)

II. And though they be born with a human body, it will be difficult for them to hear the Law, having heard which they will do penances, combat their passions and abstain from killing living beings. (8)

III. And though, by chance, they may hear the Law, it will be difficult for them to believe in it; many who are shown the right way, stray from it. (9)

IV. And though they have heard the Law and believe in it, it is difficult for them to fulfill it strenuously; many who approve of the religion, do not adopt it. (10)

Having been born as a man, having heard the Law, believing in it, and fulfilling it strenuously, an ascetic should restrain himself and shake off sinfulness. (11)

The pious obtain purity, and the pure stand firmly in the Law: (the soul afterwards) reaches the highest Nirvāṇa, being like unto a fire fed with ghee. (12)

Leave off the causes of sin, acquire fame through patience! (A man who acts up to this) will rise to the upper regions after having left this body of clay. (13)

The Yakṣas who are gifted with various virtues, (live in the heavenly regions, situated) one above the other, shining forth like the great luminaries, and hoping never to descend thence. (14)

Intent on enjoying divine pleasures and changing their form at will, they live in the upper Kalpa heavens many centuries of former[2] years. (15)

The Yakṣas, having remained there according to their merit, descend thence at the expiration of their life and are born as men.

Men are of ten kinds. (16)

Fields and houses, gold, cattle, slaves and servants: where these four goods, the causes of pleasure, are present, in such families he is born.[3] (17)

He will have friends and relations, be of good family, of fine complexion, healthy, wise, noble, famous, and powerful. (18)

After having enjoyed, at their proper time, the unrivalled pleasures of human life, he will obtain true knowledge by his pure religious merit acquired in a former life. (19)

Perceiving that the four requisites are difficult to obtain, he will apply himself to self-control, and when by penances he has shaken off the remnant of Karman, he will become an eternal Siddha. (20)

Thus I say.

Fourth Lecture: Impurity

You cannot prolong your life,[1] therefore be not careless; you are past help when old age approaches. Consider this: what (protection) will careless people get, who kill living beings and do not exert themselves? (1)

Men who adhering to wrong principles acquire wealth by evil deeds, will lose it, falling into the snares (of their passions) and being held captive by their hatred. (2)

As the burglar[2] caught in the breach of the wall perishes by the work the sinner himself had executed, thus people in this life and the next cannot escape the effect of their own actions. (3)

If a man living in the Saṃsāra does an action for the sake of somebody else, or one by which he himself also profits, then, at the time of reaping the fruit of his actions, his relations will not act as true relations (*i.e.* will not come to his help). (4)

Wealth will not protect a careless man in this world and the next. Though he had seen the right way, he does not see it, even as one in the dark whose lamp has suddenly been put out. (5)

Though others sleep, be thou awake! Like a wise man, trust nobody, but be always on the alert; for dangerous is the time and weak the body. Be always watchful like a Bhāruṇḍa[3] bird! (6)

A monk should step carefully in his walk (*i.e.* in his life), supposing everything to be a snare for him. First he must bestow care on his life till he wins the stake (*viz.* enlightenment), and afterwards he should despise it, annihilating his sins. (7)

By conquering his will, (a monk) reaches liberation, as a well-broken horse which is clad in harness (goes to battle). Be watchful in your young years; for thereby a monk quickly obtains liberation. (8)

"If he does not get (victory over his will) early, he will get it afterwards"; such reasoning[4] presupposes the eternity of human life. But such a man despairs when his life draws to its close, and the dissolution of his body approaches. (9)

One cannot quickly arrive at discernment; therefore one should exert one's self, abstain from pleasures, understand the world, be impartial like a sage, and guard one's self: (thus) never be careless. (10)

A Śramaṇa who again and again suppresses the effects of delusion, and controls himself, will be affected in a rough way by external things; but a monk should not hate them in his mind. (11)

External things weaken the intellect and allure many; therefore keep them out of your mind. Keep off delusion, remove pride, do not practise deceit, leave off greed. (12)

Heretics who are impure and vain, are always subject to love and hate, and are wholly under the influence (of their passions). Despising them as unholy men, desire virtues till the end of your life. (13)

Thus I say.

Fifth Lecture: Death Against One's Will

In this ocean (of life) with its currents (*viz.* births) difficult to cross, one man has reached the opposite shore; one wise man has given an answer to the following question. (1)

These two ways of life ending with death have been declared: death with one's will, and death against one's will. (2)

Death against one's will is that of ignorant men, and it happens (to the same individual) many times. Death with one's will is that of wise men, and at best[1] it happens but once. (3)

Mahāvīra has (thus) described the first kind in which an ignorant man, being attached to pleasures, does very cruel actions. (4)

A man attached to pleasures and amusements will be caught in the trap (of deceit). (He thinks): "I never saw the next world, but I have seen with my own eyes the pleasures of this life." (5)

"The pleasures of this life are (as it were) in your hand, but the future ones are uncertain.[2] Who knows whether there is a next world or not?" (6)

The fool boasts: "I shall have the company of (most) men."[3] But by his love of pleasures and amusements he will come to grief. (7)

Then he begins to act cruelly against movable and immovable beings, and he kills living beings with a purpose or without. (8)

An ignorant man kills, lies, deceives, calumniates, dissembles, drinks liquor, and eats meat, thinking that this is the right thing to do. (9)

Overbearing in acts and words, desirous for wealth and women, he accumulates sins in two ways,[4] just as a young snake gathers dust (both on and in its body). (10)

Then he suffers ill and is attacked by disease; and he is in dread of the next world when he reflects on his deeds. (11)

I have heard of the places in hell, and of the destination of the sinner, where the fools who do cruel deeds will suffer violently. (12)

Then going to the place where he is to be born again according to his deeds, he feels remorse, as I have heard (from my teacher). (13)

As a charioteer, who against his better judgment leaves the smooth highway and gets on a rugged road, repents when the axle breaks; so the fool, who transgresses the Law and embraces unrighteousness, repents in the hour of death, like (the charioteer) over the broken axle. (14, 15)

Then when death comes at last, the fool trembles in fear; he dies the "death against one's will," (having lost his chance) like a gambler vanquished by Kali. (16)

Thus has been explained the fools' "death against one's will"; now hear from me the wise men's "death with one's will!" (17)

Full of peace and without injury to any one is, as I have heard (from my teachers), the death of the virtuous who control themselves and subdue their senses.[5] (18)

(Such a death) does not fall to the lot of every monk, nor of every householder; for the morality of householders is of various character, and that of monks is not always good throughout. (19)

Some householders are superior to some monks in self-control; but the saints are superior to all householders in self-control. (20)

Bark and skin (of a goat), nakedness, twisted hair, baldness—these (outward tokens) will not save a sinful ascetic. (21)

A sinner, though he be a mendicant (friar), will not escape hell; but a pious man, whether monk or householder, ascends to heaven. (22)

A faithful man should practise[6] the rules of conduct for householders; he should never neglect the Pōsaha fast[7] in both fortnights, not even for a single night. (23)

When under such discipline he lives piously even as a householder, he will, on quitting flesh and bones,[8] share the world of the Yakṣas. (24)

Now a restrained monk will become one of the two: either one free from all misery or a god of great power. (25)

To the highest regions, in due order, to those where there is no delusion, and to those which are full of light, where the glorious (gods dwell)—who have long life, great power, great lustre, who can change their shape at will, who are beautiful as on their first day, and have the brilliancy of many suns—to such places go those who are trained in self-control and penance, monks or householders, who have obtained liberation by absence of passion. (26-28)

Having heard (this) from the venerable men who control themselves and subdue their senses, the virtuous and the learned do not tremble in the hour of death. (29)

A wise man having weighed (both kinds of death) and chosen the better one (taught in) the Law of Compassion, will become calm through patience, with an undisturbed mind (at the time of death). (30)

When the right time (to prepare for death) has arrived, a faithful (monk) should in the presence (of his teacher) suppress all emotions (of fear or joy) and wait for the dissolution of his body. (31)

When the time for quitting the body has come, a sage dies the "death with one's will," according to one of the three methods.[9] (32)

Thus I say.

Sixth Lecture: The False Ascetic[1]

All men who are ignorant of the Truth are subject to pain; in the endless Saṃsāra they suffer in many ways. (1)

Therefore a wise man, who considers well the ways that lead to bondage[2] and birth, should himself search for the truth, and be kind towards all creatures. (2)

"Mother, father, daughter-in-law, brother, wife, and sons will not be able to help me, when I suffer for my own deeds."[3] (3)

This truth should be taken to heart[4] by a man of pure faith; he should (therefore) cut off greed and love, and not hanker after his former connections. (4)

Cows and horses, jewels and earrings, cattle, slaves and servants: all these (possessions) you must give up in order to obtain the power of changing your form at will. (5)[5]

Everything that happens to somebody, affects him personally; therefore, knowing the creatures' love of their own self, do not deprive them of their life, but cease from endangering and combating them. (6)

Seeing that to accept (presents) leads to hell, one should not accept even a blade of grass; only to preserve one's life[6] one should eat the food that is put in one's own alms-bowl. (7)

Here some are of opinion that they will be delivered from all misery by merely attending the teacher,[7] without abstaining from sins. (8)

Acknowledging the truth about bondage and liberation, but talking only, not acting (in accordance with these tenets), they seek comfort for themselves in mighty words. (9)

Clever talking will not work salvation; how should philosophical instruction do it? Fools, though sinking lower and lower through their sins, believe themselves to be wise men. (10)

They are (going) a long way in the endless Saṃsāra; therefore looking out carefully one should wander about carefully.[8] (11)

Choosing what is beyond and above (this world, *viz.* liberation), one should never desire (worldly objects), but sustain one's body only to be able to annihilate one's Karman. (12)

Those will reap pains who, in thoughts, words, or acts, are attached to their body, to colours, and to forms. (13)

Recognising the cause of Karman, one should wander about waiting for one's death; (knowing) the permitted quantity of food and drink, one should eat (such food as has been) prepared (by the householders for their own consumption). (14)

An ascetic should not lay by any store, not even so little as the grease (sticking to his alms-bowl); but as a bird with its plumage,[9] so he with his alms-bowl should wander about without desires. (15)

Receiving alms in a manner to avoid faults,[10] and controlling one's self, one should wander about in a village (etc.) without a fixed residence; careful among the careless one should beg one's food. (16)

Thus has spoken the Arhat Jñātṛputra, the venerable native of Vaiśālī,[11] who possesses the highest knowledge and who possesses the highest faith, who possesses (at the same time) the highest knowledge and the highest faith. (17)

Thus I say.

Seventh Lecture: The Parable of the Ram, etc.

As somebody, to provide for (the arrival of) a guest, brings up a young ram, gives it rice and gram,[1] and brings it up in his yard; (1)

Then when it is grown up and big, fat and of a large belly, fattened and of a plump body, it is ready for the guest. (2)

As long as no guest comes, the poor (animal) lives; but as soon as a guest arrives, its head is cut off, and it is eaten. (3)

As this ram is well treated for the sake of a guest, even so an ignorant, great sinner longs (as it were) for life in hell. (4)

An ignorant man kills, tells lies, robs on the highway, steals foreign goods, deceives, (always thinking of some one) whom he could plunder, the villain. (5)

He is desirous of women and pleasures, he enters on undertakings and business, drinks liquor, eats meat, becomes strong, a subduer of foes. (6)

He eats crisp goats' meat, his belly grows, and his veins swell with blood—but he gains nothing but life in hell, just as the ram is only fed to be killed for the sake of a guest. (7)

After having enjoyed pleasant seats, beds, carriages, riches, and pleasures, after having squandered his wealth which he had so much trouble in gaining, and after having committed many sins, he will, under the burden of his Karman, and believing only in the visible world, be grieved in the hour of death like the ram[2] at the arrival of a guest. (8, 9)

Then the sinner who has been killing living beings, at the end of his life falls from his state,[3] and against his will he goes to the world of the Asuras, to the dark place. (10)

As a man for the sake of one Kākinī[4] (risks and) loses a thousand (Kārṣāpaṇas), or as the king lost his kingdom (and life) by eating a mango-fruit which he was strictly forbidden (by his physician):[5] (11)

Even so are human pleasures compared with the pleasures of the gods: divine life and pleasures surpass (the former) a thousand times and more. (12)

Those endowed with excellent knowledge live many nayutas[6] of years; so great a loss suffer the fools in a life of less than a hundred years! (13)

Three merchants set out on their travels, each with his capital; one of them gained there much, the second returned with his capital, and the third merchant came home after having lost his capital. This parable[7] is taken from common life; learn (to apply it) to the Law. (14, 15)

The capital is human life, the gain is heaven; through the loss of that capital man must be born as a denizen of hell or a brute animal. (16)

These are the two courses open to the sinner; they consist in misery, as corporal punishment, etc.; for the slave to his lusts[8] has forfeited human life and divine life. (17)

Having once forfeited them, he will have to endure these two states of misery; it will be difficult for him to attain an upward course[9] for a long time to come. (18)

Considering what is at stake, one should weigh (the chances of) the sinner and of the virtuous man (in one's mind).

He who brings back his capital, is (to be compared to) one who is born again as a man. (19)

Those men who through the exercise of various virtues[10] become pious householders, will be born again as men; for all beings will reap the fruit of their actions. (20)

But he who increases his capital, is (to be compared to) one who practises eminent virtues; the virtuous, excellent man cheerfully attains the state of gods.[11] (21)

When one thus knows that a (virtuous) monk or householder will be gladdened (by his gain), how, then, should a man, whilst he is losing (his chance), not be conscious of his losing it? (22)

As a drop of water at the top of a blade of Kuśa-grass dwindles down to naught when compared with the ocean, so do human pleasures when compared with divine pleasures. (23)

The pleasures in this very limited life of men are like (the water at) the top of a blade of Kuśa-grass; for the sake of what will a man not care to gain and to keep (so precious a good which he risks to lose)? (24)

He who has not renounced pleasure, will miss his aim (*i.e.* the true end of his soul); for though he has been taught the right way, he will go astray again and again. (25)

But he who has renounced pleasure, will not miss his aim; (he will think): I have learned that, by getting rid of this vile body, I shall become a god. (26)

He will be born among men where there is wealth, beauty, glory, fame, long life, and eminent happiness. (27)

See the folly of the sinner who practises unrighteousness: turning away from the Law, the great sinner will be born in hell. (28)

See the wisdom of the wise man who follows the true Law: turning away from unrighteousness, the virtuous man will be born as a god. (29)

A wise man weighs in his mind the state of the sinner and that of the virtuous man; quitting the state of the sinner, a sage realises that of the virtuous. (30)

Thus I say.

Eighth Lecture: Kapila's Verses [1]

By what acts can I escape a sorrowful lot in this unstable ineternal Saṃsāra, which is full of misery? (1)

Quitting your former connections place your affection on nothing; a monk who loves not even those who love him, will be freed from sin and hatred. (2)

Then the best of sages, who is exempt from delusion and possesses perfect knowledge and faith, speaks for the benefit and eternal welfare, and for the final liberation of all beings. (3)

All fetters (of the soul), and all hatred, everything of this kind, should a monk cast aside; he should not be attached to any pleasures, examining them well and taking care of himself. (4)

A stupid, ignorant sinner who never fixes his thoughts on the soul's benefit and eternal welfare, but sinks down through hatred and the temptation of lust, will be ensnared as a fly is caught on glue. (5)

It is difficult to cast aside the pleasures of life, weak men will not easily give them up; but there are pious ascetics (sādhu) who get over the impassable (Saṃsāra) as merchants cross the sea. (6)

Some there are who call themselves Śramaṇas, though they are like the beasts ignorant of (the prohibition of) killing living beings; the stupid sinners go to hell through their superstitious beliefs.[2] (7)

One should not permit (or consent to) the killing of living beings; then he will perhaps be delivered from all misery; thus have spoken the preceptors who have proclaimed the Law of ascetics. (8)

A careful man who does not injure living beings, is called

"circumspect" (samita). The sinful Karman will quit him as water quits raised ground. (9)

In thoughts, words, and acts he should do nothing injurious to beings who people the world, whether they move or not. (10)

He should know what alms may be accepted, and should strictly keep these rules; a monk should beg food only for the sustenance of life, and should not be dainty. (11)

He should eat what tastes badly, cold food, old beans, Vakkasa Pulāga, and for the sustenance of his life he should eat Manghu (ground badara). (12)

Those who interpret the marks of the body, and dreams, and who know the foreboding changes in the body (aṅgavidyā),[3] are not to be called Śramaṇas; thus the preceptors have declared. (13)

Those who do not take their life under discipline, who cease from meditation and ascetic practices,[4] and who are desirous of pleasures, amusements, and good fare, will be born again as Asuras. (14)

And when they rise (in another birth) from the world of the Asuras, they err about, for a long time, in the Saṃsāra; those whose souls are sullied by many sins, will hardly ever attain Bōdhi. (15)

And if somebody should give the whole earth to one man, he would not have enough; so difficult is it to satisfy anybody. (16)

The more you get, the more you want; your desires increase with your means. Though two māṣas would do to supply your want, still you would scarcely think ten millions sufficient. (17)

Do not desire (women), those female demons,[5] on whose breasts grow two lumps of flesh, who continually change their mind, who entice men, and then make a sport of them as of slaves. (18)

A houseless (monk) should not desire women, he should turn away from females; learning thoroughly the Law, a monk should strictly keep its rules. (19)

This Law has been taught by Kapila of pure knowledge; those who follow it, will be saved and will gain both worlds. (20)

Thus I say.

Ninth Lecture: The Pravrajyā of King Nami [1]

After (Nami) had descended from the world of the gods, and had been born as a man, he put an end to the influence of delusion, and remembered his former birth. (1)

Remembering his former birth, king Nami became a Svayaṃsaṃbuddha in the true Law, and placing his son on the throne he retired from the world. (2)

After having enjoyed, in the company of the beautiful ladies of his seraglio, excellent pleasures which match those of the heavens, king Nami became enlightened and gave up his pleasures. (3)

Having given up the town and country of Mithilā, his army, seraglio, and all his retinue, the venerable man retired from the world and resorted to a lonely place. (4)

When the royal Seer Nami retired from the world, at the occasion of his Pravrajyā there was an uproar in Mithilā. (5)

To the royal Seer who had reached the excellent stage of Pravrajyā, Śakra in the guise of a Brāhmaṇa addressed the following words: (6)

"Why is now Mithilā[2] full of uproar? Dreadful noises are heard from palaces and houses." (7)

On hearing this, the royal Seer Nami, pursuing his reasons and arguments, answered the king of the gods thus: (8)

"In Mithilā is the sacred[3] tree Manōrama, full of leaves, flowers, and fruits, which sheds a cool shadow; this tree is always a favourite resort of many (birds). (9)

"Now, as this sacred tree Manōrama is shaken by the storm, the birds, suffering, destitute of refuge, and miserable, scream aloud." (10)

On hearing this, the king of gods, pursuing his reasons and arguments, answered the royal Seer Nami thus: (11)

"This is fire and storm, your palace is on fire! Reverend sir, why do you not look after your seraglio?" (12)

Nami answered (see verse 8): (13)

"Happy are we, happy live we who call nothing our own; when Mithilā is on fire, nothing is burned that belongs to me. (14)

To a monk who has left his sons and wives, and who has ceased to act, nothing pleasant can occur, nor anything unpleasant. (15)

"There is much happiness for the sage, for the houseless monk, who is free from all ties, and knows himself to be single and unconnected (with the rest of the world)." (16)

Indra answered (see verse 11): (17)

"Erect a wall, gates, and battlements; dig a moat; construct śataghnīs:[4] then you will be[5] a Kṣatriya." (18)

Nami answered (see verse 8): (19)

"Making Faith his fortress, Penance and Self-control the bolt (of its gate), Patience its strong wall, so that guarded in three ways[6] it is impregnable; making Zeal his bow, its string Carefulness in walking (iriyā), and its top (where the string is fastened) Content, he should bend (this bow) with Truth, piercing with the arrow, Penance, (the foe's) mail, Karman—(in this way) a sage will be the victor in battle and get rid of the Saṃsāra." (20-22)

Indra answered (see verse 11): (23)

"Build palaces, excellent houses,[7] and turrets; thus you will be a Kṣatriya." (24)

Nami answered (see verse 8): (25)

"He who builds his house on the road, will certainly get into trouble; wherever he wants to go, there he may take up his lodgings." (26)

Indra answered (see verse 11): (27)

"Punishing thieves and robbers, cut-purses and burglars, you should establish public safety; thus you will be a Kṣatriya." (28)

Nami answered (see verse 8): (29)

"Men frequently apply punishment wrongly: the innocent are put in prison, and the perpetrator of the crime is set at liberty." (30)

Indra answered (see verse 11): (31)

"O king, bring into subjection all princes who do not acknowledge you; thus you will be a true Kṣatriya." (32)

Nami answered (see verse 8): (33)

"Though a man should conquer thousands and thousands of valiant (foes), greater will be his victory if he conquers nobody but himself. (34)

"Fight with your Self; why fight with external foes? He who conquers himself through himself, will obtain happiness. (35)

"The five senses, anger, pride, delusion, and greed—difficult to conquer is one's self; but when that is conquered, everything is conquered."[8] (36)

Indra answered (see verse 11): (37)

"Offer great sacrifices, feed Śramaṇas and Brāhmaṇas, give alms, enjoy yourself, and offer sacrifices: thus you will be a true Kṣatriya." (38)

Nami answered: (39)

"Though a man should give, every month, thousands and thousands of cows, better will be he who controls himself, though he give no alms." (40)

Indra answered: (41)

"You have left the dreadful āśrama (that of the householder)[9] and are wanting to enter another; (remain what you were), O king, and be content with observing the Pōsaha-days." (42)

Nami answered: (43)

"If an ignorant man should eat but a blade of Kuśa-grass every month, (the merit of his penance) will not equal the sixteenth part of his who possesses the Law as it has been taught." (44)

Indra answered: (45)

"Multiply your gold and silver, your jewels and pearls, your copper, fine robes, and carriages, and your treasury; then you will be a true Kṣatriya." (46)

Nami answered: (47)

"If there were numberless mountains of gold and silver, as big as Kailāsa, they would not satisfy a greedy man; for his avidity is boundless like space. (48)

"Knowing that the earth with its crops of rice and barley, with its gold and cattle, that all this put together will not satisfy one single man, one should practise austerities." (49)

Indra answered: (50)

"A miracle! O king, you give up those wonderful pleasures, in search of imaginary objects; your very hope will cause your ruin." (51)

Nami answered: (52)

"Pleasures are the thorn that rankles, pleasures are poison, pleasures are like a venomous snake; he who is desirous of pleasures will not get them, and will come to a bad end at last. (53)

"He will sink through anger; he will go down through pride; delusion will block up his path; through greed he will incur dangers in both worlds." (54)

Throwing off the guise of a Brāhmaṇa, and making visible his true form, Śakra saluted him respectfully and praised him with these sweet words: (55)

"Bravo! you have conquered anger; bravo! you have vanquished pride; bravo! you have banished delusion; bravo! you have subdued greed. (56)

"Bravo for your simplicity, O saint! bravo for your humility, O saint! bravo for your perfect patience! bravo for your perfect liberation! (57)

"Here (on earth) you are the highest man, Reverend sir, and hereafter you will be the highest; exempt from all blemishes you will reach Perfection, a higher state than which there is none in this world." (58)

Thus praising the royal Seer, Śakra in perfect faith kept his right side towards him and paid reverence to him, again and again. (59)

After having adored the best sage's feet marked by the Chakra and the Aṅkuśa,[10] he flew up through the air, with his crown and his earrings prettily trembling. (60)

Nami humbled himself; enjoined by Śakra in person, the king of Vidēha left the house, and took upon him Śramaṇahood. (61)

Thus act the enlightened, the wise, the clever ones; they turn away from pleasures, as did Nami, the royal Seer. (62)

Thus I say.

Tenth Lecture:[1] The Leaf of the Tree

As the fallow leaf of the tree falls to the ground, when its days are gone, even so the life of men (will come to its close); Gautama, be careful all the while! (1)

As a dew-drop dangling on the top of a blade of Kuśa-grass lasts but a short time, even so the life of men; Gautama, be careful all the while! (2)

As life is so fleet and existence so precarious, wipe off the sins you ever committed; Gautama, be careful all the while! (3)

A rare chance, in the long course of time, is human birth for a living being; hard are the consequences of actions; Gautama, be careful all the while! (4)

When the soul has once got into an earth-body,[2] it may remain in the same state as long as an Asaṃkhya;[3] Gautama, be careful all the while! (5)

When the soul has once got into a water-body, it may remain in the same state as long as an Asaṃkhya; Gautama, be careful all the while! (6)

When a soul has once got into a fire-body, it may remain in the same state as long as an Asaṃkhya; Gautama, be careful all the while! (7)

When the soul has once got into a wind-body, it may remain in the same state as long as an Asaṃkhya; Gautama, be careful all the while! (8)

When the soul has once got into a vegetable-body, it remains long in that state, for an endless time, after which its lot is not much bettered;[4] Gautama, be careful all the while! (9)

When the soul has once got into a body of a Dvīndriya (*i.e.* a being possessing two organs of sense), it may remain in the same state as long as a period called saṃkhyēya;[5] Gautama, be careful all the while! (10)

When the soul has once got into a body of a Trīndriya (*i.e.* a being possessing three organs of sense), it may remain in the same state as long as a period called saṃkhyēya; Gautama, be careful all the while! (11)

When the soul has once got into a body of a Chaturindriya (*i.e.* a being possessing four organs of sense), it may remain in the same state as long as a period called saṃkhyēya; Gautama, be careful all the while! (12)

When the soul has once got into a body of a Pañchēndriya (*i.e.* a being possessing five organs of sense), it may remain in the same state as long as seven or eight births; Gautama, be careful all the while! (13)

When the soul has once got into the body of a god or of a denizen of hell, it may remain in that state one whole life; Gautama, be careful all the while! (14)

Thus the soul which suffers for its carelessness, is driven about in the Saṃsāra by its good and bad Karman; Gautama, be careful all the while! (15)

Though one be born as a man, it is a rare chance to become an ārya; for many are the Dasyus and Mlēcchas; Gautama, be careful all the while! (16)

Though one be born as an ārya, it is a rare chance to possess all five organs of sense; for we see many who lack one organ or other; Gautama, be careful all the while! (17)

Though he may possess all five organs of sense, still it is a rare chance to be instructed in the best Law; for people follow heretical teachers; Gautama, be careful all the while! (18)

Though he may have been instructed in the right Law, still it is a rare chance to believe in it; for many people are heretics; Gautama, be careful all the while! (19)

Though one believe in the Law, he will rarely practise it; for people are engrossed by pleasures; Gautama, be careful all the while! (20)

When your body grows old, and your hair turns white, the power of your ears decreases; Gautama, be careful all the while! (21)

When your body grows old, and your hair turns white, the power of your eyes decreases; Gautama, be careful all the while! (22)

When your body grows old, and your hair turns white, the power of your nose decreases. (23)

When your body grows old, and your hair turns white, the power of your tongue decreases. (24)

When your body grows old, and your hair turns white, the power of your touch decreases. (25)

When your body grows old, and your hair turns white, all your powers decrease. (26)

Despondency, the king's evil, cholera, mortal diseases of many kinds befall you; your body wastes and decays; Gautama, be careful all the while! (27)

Cast aside from you all attachments, as the(leaves of) a lotus let drop off the autumnal[6] water, exempt from every attachment, Gautama, be careful all the while! (28)

Give up your wealth and your wife; you have entered the state of the houseless; do not, as it were, return to your vomit; Gautama, be careful all the while! (29)

Leave your friends and relations, the large fortune you have amassed; do not desire them a second time; Gautama, be careful all the while! (30)

There is now no Jina,[7] but there is a highly esteemed guide to show the way; now being on the right path, Gautama, be careful all the while! (31)

Now you have entered on the path from which the thorns have been cleared, the great path; walk in the right path; Gautama, etc. (32)

Do not get into an uneven road like a weak burden-bearer; for you will repent of it afterwards; Gautama, be careful all the while! (33)

You have crossed the great ocean; why do you halt so near the shore? make haste to get on the other side; Gautama, be careful all the while! (34)

Going through the same religious practices as perfected saints,[8] you will reach the world of perfection, Gautama, where there is safety and perfect happiness; Gautama, be careful all the while! (35)

The enlightened[9] and liberated monk should control himself, whether he be in a village or a town, and he should preach to all[10] the road of peace; Gautama, be careful all the while! (36)

Having heard the Buddha's[11] well-delivered sermon, adorned by illustrations, Gautama cut off love and hatred and reached perfection. (37) Thus I say.

Eleventh Lecture: The Very Learned

I shall explain, in due order, the right discipline of a houseless monk who has got rid of all worldly ties. Listen to me. (1)

He who is ignorant of the truth, egoistical, greedy, without self-discipline, and who talks loosely, is called ill-behaved and void of learning. (2)

There are five causes which render wholesome discipline impossible: egoism, delusion, carelessness, illness, and idleness: (3)

For eight causes discipline is called virtue, *viz*.: not to be fond of mirth, to control one's self, not to speak evil of others, not to be without discipline, not to be of wrong discipline, not to be covetous, not to be choleric, to love the truth; for their influence discipline is called virtue. (4, 5)

A monk who is liable to the following fourteen charges, is called ill-behaved, and does not reach Nirvāṇa: (6)

If he is frequently angry; if he perseveres in his wrath; if he spurns friendly advice; if he is proud of his learning; if he finds fault with others; if he is angry even with friends; if he speaks evil even of a good friend behind his back; if he is positive in his assertions; if he is malicious, egoistical, greedy, without self-discipline; if he does not share with others; if he is always unkind: then he is called ill-behaved. (7-9)

But for the following fifteen good qualities he is called well-behaved: if he is always humble, steady, free from deceit and curiosity; if he abuses nobody; if he does not persevere in his wrath,; if he listens to friendly advice; if he is not proud of his learning; if he does not find fault with others; if he is not angry with friends; if he speaks well even of a bad friend behind his back; if he abstains from quarrels and rows; if he is enlightened, polite, decent, and quiet: then he is called well-behaved. (10-13)

He who always acknowledges his allegiance to his teacher,[1] who has religious zeal and ardour for study, who is kind in words and actions, deserves to be instructed. (14)

As water put into a shell shines with a doubled brilliancy, so do the piety, fame, and knowledge of a very learned monk. (15)

As a trained Kambōja-steed, whom no noise frightens,[2] exceeds all other horses in speed, so a very learned monk is superior to all others.[3] (16)

As a valiant hero bestriding a trained horse, with heralds singing out to his right and left, (has no equal),[4] neither has a very learned monk. (17)

As a strong and irresistible elephant of sixty years, surrounded by his females, (has no equal), neither has a very learned monk. (18)

As a sharp-horned, strong-necked bullock, the leader of the herd, is a fine sight, so is a very learned monk. (19)

As a proud lion with sharp fangs, who brooks no assault, is superior to all animals, so is a very learned monk (superior to all men). (20)

As Vāsudēva, the god with the conch, discus, and club, who fights with an irresistible strength, (has no equal), neither has a very learned monk. (21)

As a universal monarch with his fourfold army and great power, the possessor of the fourteen attributes of a king, (has no equal), neither has a very learned monk. (22)

As Śakra the thousand-eyed, the wielder of the thunderbolt, the fortress-destroyer, the king of gods, (has no equal), neither has a very learned monk. (23)

As the rising sun, the dispeller of darkness, who burns as it were with light, (has no equal), neither has a very learned monk. (24)

As the moon, the queen of the stars, surrounded by the asterisms, when she is full at full-moon, (has no equal), neither has a very learned monk. (25)

As a well-guarded storehouse of merchants, which is filled with grain of many kinds, (has no equal), neither has a very learned monk. (26)

As the best of Jambū[5] trees, called Sudarśanā, which is the abode of the presiding deity, (has no equal), neither has a very learned monk. (27)

As the best of rivers, the ocean-flowing stream Śītā[6] with its dark waters, (has no equal), neither has a very learned monk. (28)

As the best of hills, high mount Mandara, on which various plants shed a bright lustre, (has no equal), neither has a very learned monk. (29)

As the ocean of inexhaustible water, the delight of Svayambhū,[7] which is full of precious things of many kinds, (has no equal), neither has a very learned monk. (30)

Monks who equal the ocean in depth, who are difficult to overcome, are frightened by nobody (or nothing), and are not easily assailed, who are full of extensive learning and take care of themselves, will go to the highest place, after their Karman has been annihilated. (31)

Therefore, seeker after the highest truth, study the sacred lore, in order to cause yourself and others to attain perfection. (32)

Thus I say.

Twelfth Lecture:[1] Harikēśa

Harikēśa-Bala was born in a family of Śvapākas (Chāṇḍālas); he became a monk and a sage, possessed of the highest virtues, who had subdued his senses. (1)

He observed the rules with regard to walking, begging, speaking, easing nature, and receiving and keeping (of things necessary for a monk)[2] controlled himself, and was always attentive (to his duty). (2)

He protected from sin his thoughts, speech, and body,[3] and subdued his senses.

Once on his begging tour, he approached the enclosure of a Brahmanical sacrifice. (3)

When(the priests) saw him coming up, emaciated by austerities, in a miserable condition, and with the poorest outfit, they laughed at him, the ruffians. (4)

Stuck up by pride of birth, those killers of animals, who did not subdue their senses, the unchaste sinners, made the following speech: (5)

"Who is that dandy coming there? he is swarthy, dreadful, with a turned-up nose, miserably clad, a very devil[4] of a dirty man, with a filthy cloth put on his neck? (6)

"Who are you, you monster? or for what purpose have you come here? you miserably clad devil of a dirty man! go, get away! why stand you there?" (7)

At this turn the Yakṣa, who lived in the Tinduka-tree, had compassion on the great sage, and making his own body invisible spoke the following words: (8)

"I am a chaste Śramaṇa, controlling myself; I have no property, nothing belonging to me, and do not cook my food; I have come for food which is dressed for somebody else at the time when I call. (9)

"You give away, eat, and consume plenty of food; know that I subsist by begging; let the mendicant get what is left of the rest." (10)

"The dinner has been prepared for Brāhmaṇas, it has been got ready especially for ourselves and for us exclusively; we shall not give you such food and drink; why stand you there?" (11)

"The husbandmen throw the corn on high ground and on low ground,[5] hoping (for a return). For the like motive give unto me; I may be the field which may produce merit (as the return for your benevolence)." (12)

"All the world knows that we are (as it were) the field on which gifts sown grow up as merit; Brāhmaṇas of pure birth and knowledge are the blessed fields." (13)

"Those who are full of anger and pride, who kill, lie, steal, and own property, are Brāhmaṇas without pure birth and knowledge; they are very bad fields. (14)

"You are only the bearer of words as it were, you do not understand their meaning, though you have learned the Vēdas. The saints call at high and lowly (houses); they are the blessed fields." (15)

"Detractor of the learned doctors, how dare you speak thus in our presence! This food and drink should rather rot, than we should give it you, Nirgrantha."[6] (16)

"If you do not give me what I ask for, I who observe the Samitis, who am protected by the Guptis,[7] who subdue my senses, what benefit, then, will you gain by your sacrifices?" (17)

"Are here no Kṣatriyas, no priests who tend the fire, no teachers with their disciples, who will beat him with a stick, or pelt him with a nut, take him by the neck, and drive him off?" (18)

On these words of the teachers, many young fellows rushed forward, and they all beat the sage with sticks, canes, and whips. (19)

At that turn king Kausalika's daughter, Bhadrā, of faultless body, saw that the monk was beaten, and appeased the angry youngsters. (20)

"He is the very man to whom the king, impelled by the devil (who possessed me), had given me, but who would not think of me; he is the sage whom princes and gods adore, who has refused me. (21)

"He is that austere ascetic, of noble nature, who subdues his senses and controls himself; the chaste man, who would not accept me when my own father, king Kausalika, gave me to him. (22)

"He is the man of great fame and might, of awful piety and power; do not injure him who cannot be injured, lest he consume you all by the fire (of his virtue)." (23)

When the Yakṣas heard these well-spoken words of (the Purōhita's) wife Bhadrā, they came to the assistance of the sage, and kept the young men off. (24)

Appearing in the air with hideous shapes, the Asuras beat the people. When Bhadrā saw them with rent bodies spitting blood, she spoke again thus: (25)

"You may as well dig rocks with your nails, or eat iron with your teeth, or kick fire with your feet, as treat contemptuously a monk. (26)

"Like a poisonous snake is a great sage of severe austerities, of tremendous piety and power; like a swarm of moths you will rush into a fire, if you beat a monk on his begging tour. (27)

"Prostrate yourself before him for protection, you together with all of them, if you want to save your life and your property; for in his wrath he might reduce the world to ashes." (28)

When the Brāhmaṇa saw the disciples bowing their back and head, and holding out their hands, not minding their occupation; with streaming eyes, spitting blood, looking upwards, their eyes and tongues protruding, like as many logs of wood, he became heartbroken and dejected, and together with his wife he appeased the sage: "Forgive us our injury and abuse, sir! (29, 30)

"Forgive, sir, these ignorant, stupid boys, that they injured you; sages are exceedingly gracious, nor are the saints inclined to wrath." (31)

"There is not the least hatred in me, neither now, nor before, nor in future. The Yakṣas attend upon me, therefore they have beaten the boys." (32)

"You know the truth and the Law; you are not angry, compassionate sage; we take refuge at your feet, we together with all of them. (33)

"We worship you, mighty sir; there is nothing in you that we do not worship; eat this dish of boiled rice seasoned with many condiments. (34)

"I have got plenty of food; eat it to do us a favour!" The noble (monk) said "yes," and took food and drink after having fasted a whole month. (35)

At that moment the gods caused a rain of perfumed water and flowers, and showered down heavenly treasures; they struck the drums, and in the air they praised the gift. (36)

"The value of penance has become visible, birth appears of no value! Look at the holy Harikēśa, the son of a Śvapāka, whose power is so great." (37)

"O Brāhmaṇas, why do you tend the fire, and seek external purity by water? The clever ones say that external purity which you seek for, is not the right thing. (38)

"You (use) Kuśa-grass, sacrificial poles, straw and wood, you touch water in the evening and in the morning; thereby you injure living beings, and in your ignorance you commit sins again and again." (39)

"How should we sacrifice, O monk, and how avoid sinful actions? Tell us, ascetic, whom the Yakṣas hold in honour, what do the clever ones declare to be the right method of sacrificing?" (40)

"Doing no injury to living beings of the six orders, abstaining from lying and from taking what is not freely given, renouncing property, women, pride, and deceit, men should live under self-restraint. (41)

"He who is well protected by the five Saṃvaras[8] and is not attached to this life, who abandons his body,[9] who is pure and does not care for his body, wins the great victory, the best of offerings." (42)

"Where is your fire, your fireplace, your sacrificial ladle? where the dried cowdung (used as fuel)? Without these things, what kind of priests can the monks be? What oblations do you offer to the fire? (43)

"Penance is my fire; life my fireplace; right exertion is my sacrificial ladle; the body the dried cowdung; Karman is my fuel; self-control, right exertion, and tranquillity are the oblations, praised by the sages, which I offer." (44)

"Where is your pond, and where the holy bathing-place? how do you make your ablutions or get rid of impurity? Tell us, O restrained monk whom the Yakṣas hold in honour; we desire to learn it from you." (45)

"The Law is my pond, celibacy my holy bathing-place, which is not turbid, and throughout clear for the soul;[10] there I make ablutions; pure, clean, and thoroughly cooled I get rid of hatred[11] (or impurity). (46)

"The clever ones have discovered such bathing, it is the great bath praised by the seers, in which the great seers bathe, and, pure and clean, they obtain the highest place." (47)

Thus I say.

Thirteenth Lecture: Chitra and Sambhūta [1]

Being contemptuously treated for the sake of his birth (as a Chāṇḍāla) Sambhūta took, in Hastināpura, the sinful resolution (to become a universal monarch in some later birth); descending from the heavenly region Padmagulma, he was born of Chulanī in Kāmpilya as Brahmadatta; Chitra, however, was born in the town Purimatāla in the great family of a merchant; when he had heard the Law, he entered the order. (1, 2)

In the town Kāmpilya, both Sambhūta and Chitra (as they were called in a former birth) met again and told each other the reward they had realised for their good and bad actions. (3)

The universal monarch Brahmadatta, the powerful and glorious king, respectfully addressed the following words to him (who had been) his brother (in a former birth): (4)

We were brothers once, kind to each other, loving each other, wishing well to each other. (5)

"We were slaves in the country of the Daśārṇas, then antelopes on mount Kālañjara, then geese on the shore of Mṛtagaṅgā, and Śvapākas in the land of Kāśi. (6)

"And we were gods having great power, in the regions of the gods. This is our sixth birth, in which we are separated from each other." (7)

"Karman is produced by sinful thoughts, and you have entertained them, O king; it is by the influence of this Karman that we were separated." (8)

"I had done actions derived from truth and purity, and now I enjoy their effect; is this also true in your case, Chitra?" (9)

"Every good deed will bear its fruit to men; there is no escape from the effect of one's actions. Through riches and the highest pleasures my soul has got the reward for its virtues. (10)

"Know, Sambhūta, that you have got the reward of your virtues in the shape of great wealth and prosperity; but know, O king, that is just so with Chitra; he also obtained prosperity and splendour. (11)

"A song of deep meaning condensed in words has been repeated in the midst of a crowd of men, (having heard) which monks of piety and virtues exert themselves in this (religion): I have become a Śramaṇa." (12)

"Renowned are my beautiful palaces Ucca, Udaya, Madhu, Karka, and Brahman: this house, full of treasures and containing the finest products of the Pañchālas, O Chitra,[2] regard it as your own! (13)

"Surround yourself with women who dance, and sing, and make music; enjoy these pleasures, O monk; I deem renunciation a hard thing." (14)

As the virtuous Chitra, for old friendship's sake, loved the king who was attached to sensual pleasures, and as he had at heart his welfare, he spoke to him the following words: (15)

"All singing is but prattle, all dancing is but mocking, all ornaments are but a burden, all pleasures produce but pains. (16)

"O king, pleasures which the ignorant like, but which produce pains, do not delight pious monks who care not for pleasure, but are intent on the virtues of right conduct. (17)

"Excellent king, the lowest caste of men is that of the Śvapākas, to which we twice belonged; as such we were loathed by all people, and we lived in the hamlets of Śvapākas. (18)

"In that miserable birth we lived in the hamlets of Śvapākas, detested by all people; then we acquired the Karman (the fruit of which we now enjoy). (19)

"You are now a king of great power and prosperity, enjoying the reward of your good actions; put from you the transitory pleasures, and enter the order for the sake of the highest good![3] (20)

"He who in this life has done no good actions and has not practised the Law, repents of it in the next world when he has become a prey to

Death. (21)

"As a lion takes hold of an antelope, so Death leads off a man in his last hour; neither mother, nor father, nor brother will, at that time, save a particle (of his life). (22)

"Neither his kinsmen, nor his friends, nor his sons, nor his relations will share his suffering, he alone has to bear it; for the Karman follows the doer. (23)

"Leaving behind bipeds and quadrupeds, his fields, his house, his wealth, his corn, and everything; against his will, and accompanied only by his Karman,[4] he enters a new existence, either a good or a bad one. (24)

"When they have burned with fire on the funeral pile his forlorn, helpless corpse, his wife and sons and kinsfolk will choose another man to provide for them. (25)

"Life drags on (towards death) continuously;[5] old age carries off the vigour of man. King of the Pañchālas, mark my words: do no fearful actions." (26)

"I, too, know just as well as you, O saint, what you have told me in your speech: pleasures will get a hold on men and are not easily abandoned by such as we are, sir. (27)

"O Chitra, in Hastināpura[6] I saw the powerful king (Sanatkumāra), and I took that sinful resolution in my desire for sensual pleasures. (28)

And since I did not repent of it, this has come of it, that I still long for sensual pleasures, though I know the Law. (29)

"As an elephant, sinking down in a quagmire, sees the raised ground but does not get to the shore, so do we who long for sensual pleasures, not follow the path of monks. (30)

"Time elapses and quickly pass the days; the pleasures of men are not permanent; they come to a man and leave him just as a bird leaves a tree void of fruit." (31)

"If you are unable to abandon pleasure, then do noble actions, O king; following the Law, have compassion on all creatures: then you will become a god on entering a new existence. (32)

"If you have no intention of abandoning pleasure, and still long for undertakings and property, my long talk has been to no purpose. I go, king, farewell." (33)

And Brahmadatta, king of the Pañchālas, did not act on the counsel of the saint; he enjoyed the highest pleasure, and (afterwards) sank into the deepest hell. (34)

But Chitra the great sage, of excellent conduct and penance, was indifferent to pleasure; after he had practised the highest self-control, he reached the highest place of perfection. (35)

Thus I say.

Fourteenth Lecture: Iṣukāra

Having been gods in a former existence and lived in the same heavenly region, some were born (here below) in the ancient, wealthy, and famous town called Iṣukāra,[1] which is beautiful like heaven. (1)

By a remnant of the merit they had acquired in their former life, they were born in noble families. Disgusted with the world and afraid of the Saṃsāra, they abandoned (pleasures, etc.) and took refuge in the path of the Jinas. (2)

Two males remained bachelors, (the third became) the Purōhita (Bhṛgu), (the fourth) his wife Yaśā, (the fifth) the widely-famed king Iṣukāra, and (the sixth) his wife Kamalāvatī. (3)

Overcome by fear of birth, old age, and death, their mind intent on pilgrimage, and hoping to escape the Wheel of Births, they examined pleasures and abandoned them. (4)

Both dear sons of the Brahmanical Purōhita, who was intent on works, remembered their former birth, and the penance and self-control they had then practised. (5)

Averse to human and heavenly pleasures, desiring liberation, and full of faith, they went to their father and spoke thus: (6)

"Seeing that the lot of man is transitory and precarious, and that his life lasts not long, we take no delight in domestic life; we bid you farewell: we shall turn monks." (7)

In order to dissuade them from a life of austerities, the father replied to those (would-be) monks: "Those versed in the Vēdas say that there will be no better world for men without sons. (8)

"My sons, after you have studied the Vēdas, and fed the priests, after you have placed your own sons at the head of your house, and after you have enjoyed life together with your wives, then you may depart to the woods as praiseworthy sages." (9)

The young men perceiving that the Purōhita was wholly consumed, as it were, by the fire of grief, which was fed by his individual inclinations and blown into a huge flame by the wind of delusion; that he suffered much and talked a great deal in many ways; that he tried to persuade them by degrees, and that he would even bribe them with money and with objects of desire, (spoke) these words: (10, 11)

"The study of the Vēdas will not save you; the feeding of Brāhmaṇas will lead you from darkness to darkness, and the birth of sons will not save you. Who will assent to what you said? (12)

"Pleasures bring only a moment's happiness, but suffering for a very long time, intense suffering, but slight happiness; they are an obstacle to the liberation from existence, and are a very mine of evils. (13)

"While a man walks about without abandoning pleasures, and grieves day and night, while he is anxious about other people, and seeks for wealth, he comes to old age and death. (14)

"I have this, and I have not that; I must do this, and I should not do that! While he talks in this strain, the robbers (*viz.* time) drag him away. What foolishness is this!" (15)

"Great wealth and women, a family and exquisite pleasures: for such things people practise austerities. All this you may have for your asking." (16)

"What avail riches for the practice of religion, what a family, what pleasures? We shall become "As fire is produced in the Araṇi-wood, as butter in milk, and oil in sesamum seed, so, my sons, is the soul[2] produced in the body; (all these things) did not exist before, they came into existence, and then they perish; but they are not permanent." (18)

"(The soul) cannot be apprehended by the senses, because it possesses no corporeal form,[3] and since it possesses no corporeal form it is eternal. The fetter of the soul has been ascertained to be caused by its bad qualities, and this fetter is called the cause of worldly existence. (19)

"Thus being ignorant of the Law, we formerly did sinful actions, and through our wrong-mindedness we were kept back and retained (from entering the order). We shall not again act in the same way. (20)

"As mankind is harassed (by the one), and taken hold of (by the other), and as the unfailing ones go by, we take no delight in the life of a householder." (21)

"Who harasses the world? who takes hold of it? whom do you call unfailing? My sons, I am anxious to learn this." (22)

"Mankind is harassed by Death; it is taken hold of by Old Age; the days[4] are called unfailing: know this, Father! (23)

"The day that goes by will never return; the days elapse without profit to him who acts contrary to the Law. (24)

"The day that goes by will never return; the days elapse with much profit to him who acts up to the Law." (25)

"Having lived together in one place, and both parties[5] having acquired righteousness, we shall, O my sons, afterwards go forth (as monks) and beg alms from house to house." (26)

"He who can call Death his friend, or who can escape him, or who knows that he will not die, might perhaps decide: this shall be done tomorrow. (27)

"We will even now adopt the Law, after the adoption of which we shall not be born again. The future has nothing in store for us (which we have not experienced already). Faith will enable us to put aside attachment." (28)

(Bhṛgu speaks to his wife Vāsiṣṭhī.) "Domestic life ceases (to have attraction) for one who has lost his sons; Vāsiṣṭhī, the time has arrived for me to turn mendicant friar. As long as a tree retains its branches, it is really a tree; when they are lopped off, it is called a trunk. (29)

"As a bird without its wings, as a king in battle without his followers, as a merchant on a boat without his goods, even so am I without my sons." (30)

"You have brought together all these objects of desire, and have collected many exquisitely pleasant things. Let us, therefore, fully enjoy the pleasures; afterwards we shall go forth on the road of salvation." (31)

"We have finished enjoying pleasures, my dear; our life is drawing to its close. I do not abandon pleasures for the sake of an unholy life; but looking with indifference on gain and loss, on happiness and suffering, I shall lead the life of a monk." (32)

"May you not remember your brothers (when it is too late) like an old goose swimming against the current. Enjoy the pleasures together with me. A mendicant's life is misery." (33)

"My dear, as a snake casts off the slough of its body and goes along free and easy, even so have my sons abandoned pleasure. Why should I, being left alone, not follow them? (34)

"As the fish Rōhita[6] breaks through a weak net, even so wise men of exemplary character and famous for their austerities abandon pleasure and live as mendicants. (35)

"As the herons fly through the air and the geese too, who had rent the net, even so my sons and my husband depart. Why should I, being left alone, not follow them?" (36)

When the queen had heard that the Purōhita with his wife and sons had entered the order, abandoning pleasures and all his large property, she spoke to the king: (37)

"A man who returns, as it were,. to the vomit, is not praised; but you want to confiscate[7] the property left by the Brāhmaṇa. (38)

"If the whole world and all treasures were yours, you would still not be satisfied, nor would all this be able to save you. (39)

"Whenever you die, O king, and leave all pleasant things behind, the Law alone, and nothing else in this world, will save you, O monarch. (40)

"As a bird dislikes the cage, so do I (dislike the world). I shall live as a nun, without offspring, poor, upright, without desire, without love of gain, and without hatred. (42)

"As when by a conflagration of a forest animals are burned, other beasts greatly rejoice, being under the influence of love and hate; even so we, fools that we are, being attached to pleasure, do not perceive that the world is consumed by the fire of love and hatred. (42, 43)

"Those who have enjoyed pleasures, and have renounced them, move about like the wind, and go wherever they please, like the birds unchecked in their flight. (44)

"When they[8] are caught, and held by my hand, sir, they struggle; we shall be like them, if we are attached to pleasures. (45)

"As an unbaited (bird)[9] sees a baited one caught in the snare, even so shall we avoid every bait and walk about, not baited by anything. (46)

"Being aware that pleasures are causes for the continuance of worldly existence, as illustrated in (the above) similes of the greedy man, one should be cautious and stir as little as possible, like a snake in the presence of Suparṇa. (47)

"Like an elephant who has broken his fetters, go to your proper destination. O great king Iṣukāri; this is the wholesome truth I have learned. (48)

"Leave your large kingdom and the pleasures which are so dear to all; abandon what pleases the senses, and what attracts; be without attachment and property; learn thoroughly the Law and give up all amusements; then practise famous and severe penance, being of firm energy."[10] (49, 50)

In this way all (these) professors of the Law gradually obtained enlightenment, being frightened by birth and death, and seeking for the end of misery. (51)

Their doubts about the true doctrine were dispersed, and they realised the Bhāvanās;[11] in a short time they reached the end of misery. (52)

The king and the queen, the Brahmanical Purōhita, his wife, and his sons, they all reached perfection. (53)

Thus I say.

Fifteenth Lecture: The True Monk[1]

He who adopts the Law in the intention to live as a monk, should live in company (with other monks), upright, and free from desire; he should abandon his former connections, and not longing for pleasures, he should wander about as an unknown beggar: then he is a true monk. (1)

Free from love he should live, a model of righteousness,[2] abstaining from sins, versed in the sacred lore, protecting his soul (from every wrong), wise, hardy, observing everything; he who is attached to nothing, is a true monk. (2)

Ignorant of abuse and injury, a steadfast monk should be a model of righteousness, always protecting his soul (from sins), neither rash nor passionate; when he endures everything, then he is a true monk. (3)

He who is content with lowly beds and lodgings, bears heat and cold, flies and gnats, is neither rash nor passionate, and endures everything, he is a true monk. (4)

He does not expect respectful treatment, nor hospitality, nor reverence, nor, indeed, praises; he controls himself, keeps the vows, practises austerities, lives together with other monks, meditates on his soul; this is a true monk. (5)

If he does not care for his life, or abandons every delusion, if he avoids men and women, always practises austerities, and does not betray any curiosity, then he is a true monk. (6)

He who does not profess and live on divination from cuts and shreds,[3] from sounds on the earth or in the air, from dreams, from diagrams, sticks, and properties of buildings, from changes in the body, from the meaning[4] of the cries (of animals)—he is a true monk. (7)

Spells, roots, every kind of medical treatment, emetics, purgatives, fumigation, anointing of the eye, and bathing, the patient's lamentation, and his consolation—he who abstains from all these things, is a true monk. (8)

He who does not praise, or pay attention to, the warriors, Ugras,[5] princes, Brāhmaṇas, Bhōgas, and artists of all sorts, who abstains from this, he is a true monk. (9)

He who does not, for earthly gain, improve his acquaintance with householders, with whom he fell in as a monk, or was in friendly relation before that time, he is a true monk. (10)

A Nirgrantha is forbidden to take from householders, if they do not give it themselves, bed, lodging, drink, food, or any dainties and spices; he who is not angry at such occasions, he is a true monk. (11)

If a monk gets any food and drink, or dainties and spices, and does not feel compassion (on a sick fellow-monk) in thoughts, words, and deeds, (then he is not a true monk);[6] but if he has his thoughts, words, and acts under strict discipline, then he is a true monk. (12)

Dish-water,[7] barley-pap, cold sour gruel,[8] water in which barley has been washed: such loathsome food and drink he should not despise, but call at the lowliest houses (for alms); then he is a true monk. (13)

There are many voices on the earth, of gods, of men, and of beasts, dreadful, frightful, and awful noises; if he hears them without trembling, then he is a true monk. (14)

He who understands all religious disputations, [who lives together with fellow-monks],[9] who practises self-discipline,[10] who meditates on his soul, who is wise, hardy, and observes everything, who is calm, and does not hurt anybody, he is a true monk. (15)

He who, not living by any art, without house, without friends, subduing his senses, free from all ties, sinless, and eating but little, leaves the house and lives single, he is a true monk. (16)

Thus I say.

Sixteenth Lecture: The Ten Conditions of Perfect Chastity

O long-lived (Gambūsvāmin)! I (Sudharman) have heard the following Discourse from the Venerable (Mahāvīra):

Here,[1] indeed, the venerable Sthaviras have declared ten conditions for the realisation of celibacy, by hearing and understanding which the monks will reach a high degree of self-discipline, of Saṃvara,[2] and of contemplation, will be well protected (by the three Guptis), will guard their senses, guard their chastity, and will thus never be remiss (in the attendance on their religious duties).

What, then, are those ten conditions for the realisation of celibacy as declared by the venerable Sthaviras, by hearing and understanding which the monks will reach a high degree of self-discipline, of Saṃvara, and of contemplation, will be well protected (by the three Guptis), will guard their senses, guard their chastity, and will thus never be remiss (in the attendance on their religious duties)?

These, then, are the ten conditions for the realisation of celibacy, etc. (all down to) duties.

1. A Nirgrantha may occupy various places for sleep or rest;[3] but a Nirgrantha should not occupy places, for sleep or rest, frequented by women, cattle, or eunuchs. The preceptor has explained the reason for this. If a Nirgrantha occupies places for sleep or rest, frequented by women, cattle, or eunuchs, then, though he be chaste, there may arise a doubt with regard to his chastity, or a sensual desire, or a feeling of remorse, or he will break the rules, or he will become a slave to passion,

or he will acquire a dangerous illness of long duration, or he will desert the faith which the Kēvalin has proclaimed. Therefore a Nirgrantha should not occupy places, for sleep or rest, frequented by women, cattle, or eunuchs.

2. A Nirgrantha should not converse with women.[4] The preceptor has explained the reason for this. If a Nirgrantha converses with women, etc. (all as above).

3. A Nirgrantha should not sit together with women on the same seat. The preceptor has explained the reason for this. If a Nirgrantha sits on the same seat with women, etc. (all as above).

4. A Nirgrantha should not look at, or contemplate, the charms and beauties of women. (The rest similar as above.)

5. A Nirgrantha should not, behind a screen, or curtain, or wall, listen to the screeching or screaming or singing or laughing or giggling or crying of women. (The rest similar as above.)

6. A Nirgrantha should not recall to his memory the pleasure and amusements which in the past he enjoyed together with women. (The rest similar as above.)

7. A Nirgrantha should not eat well-dressed food. (The rest similar as above.)

8. A Nirgrantha should not eat or drink to excess. (The rest similar as above.)

9. A Nirgrantha should not wear ornaments. The preceptor has explained the reason for this. If he wears ornaments, or adorns his body, he might become an object of desire to women. When he is an object of desire to women, then, etc. (the rest as in 1).

10. A Nirgrantha should not care for sounds, colours, tastes, smells, and feelings. (The rest similar as above.)

Here are some verses (to the same effect):[5]

A monk should take up a detached lodging, free from, and not frequented by women, to preserve his chastity. (1)

A chaste monk should avoid talking with women, which delights the mind and foments love and passion. (2)

A chaste monk should always avoid the company of, and frequent conversation with women. (3)

A chaste monk should avoid observing the body, limbs, and figure of women, their pleasant prattle and oglings. (4)

A chaste monk should avoid listening to the screeching, screaming, singing, laughing, giggling, and crying of women. (5)

A chaste monk should never recall to his mind how he had laughed and played with women, and had enjoyed them, how they became jealous, and what tricks he played to frighten them. (6)

A chaste monk should always avoid well-dressed food and drink which will soon raise his sensuality. (7)

A chaste monk should always eat his food, collected according to the rules, for the sustenance of life, in the prescribed quantity, and at the right time; concentrated in his thoughts he should not eat to excess. (8)

A chaste monk should abstain from ornaments, he should not adorn his body after the fashion of amorous people. (9)

He should always abstain from the five orders of pleasant things: sounds, colours, smells, tastes, and feelings of touch. (10)

A lodging frequented by women, their pleasant talk, their company, and looking at their charms; (11)

Their screeching, screaming, singing, and laughing, eating and sleeping together with them; well-dressed food and drink, or partaking of them to excess; (12)

And ornaments and finery:[6] these pleasant things, which are hard to leave, are like the poison Tālapuṭa,[7] for a man who seeks after the true Self. (13)

He should, once for all, abandon pleasant things which are hard to leave; and concentrated in his thoughts he should avoid whatever casts a doubt on his chastity. (14)

A monk should be the steadfast charioteer, as it were, of the Law in the park of the Law,[8] a vessel of righteousness, content, restrained, attentive to the duties of a chaste monk. (15)

The gods, Dānavas, Gandharvas, Yakṣas, Rākṣasas, and Kinnaras pay homage to a chaste monk who performs his difficult duties. (16)

This unchangeable, permanent, and eternal Law has been proclaimed by the Jinas; through it the Siddhas have reached perfection, and others will reach it. (17)

Thus I say.

Seventeenth Lecture: The Bad Sramana

A Nirgrantha who has entered the order, who has learned the Law, who has received religious discipline, and who has obtained the benefit of Bōdhi which is difficult to obtain, may perhaps afterwards begin to live as he likes. (1)

(He will say:) I have a good bed and wherewithal to cover me; I obtain food and drink; I know everything that comes to pass, friend; why then should I study, sir? (2)

He who, after entering the order, always sleeps, eats, and drinks as much as he likes, and lives comfortably, is called a bad Śramaṇa. (3)

The sinner who despises the learning and discipline which his preceptor and teachers have taught him, is called a bad Śramaṇa. (4)

He who does not, as he should, strive to please his preceptor and teachers, and does not, in his arrogance, treat them with respect, is called a bad Śramaṇa. (5)

He who hurts living beings, seeds, and sprouts, who does not control himself, though he believes himself well-controlled, is called a bad Śramaṇa. (6)

He who uses a bed, a plank, a chair, a seat, or his duster,[1] without having well wiped these things, is called a bad Śramaṇa. (7)

He who walks with great haste and without care, being overbearing and fierce, is called a bad Śramaṇa. (8)

He who carelessly inspects things,[2] throwing down his duster at random, not being attentive to the inspection of things, is called a bad Śramaṇa. (9)

He who carelessly inspects things, his attention being absorbed by what he hears, who always slights his teachers, is called a bad Śramaṇa. (10)

He who is deceitful, talkative, arrogant, greedy, who does not control himself, nor share (his food, etc. with those who are in want), and is not of an amiable disposition, is called a bad Śramaṇa. (11)

He who is a controversialist, and ill-behaved, who perverts the truth, and delights in quarrels and contentions, is called a bad Śramaṇa. (12)

He who sits down on a weak, shaking seat wherever he lists, and is not careful in sitting down, is called a bad Śramaṇa. (13)

He who sleeps with dusty feet and does not inspect his couch, being careless about his bed, is called a bad Śramaṇa. (14)

He who eats milk, curds, and other things produced from milk, and does not practise austerities, is called a bad Śramaṇa. (15)

He who eats after sunset, and when admonished, makes an angry reply, is called a bad Śramaṇa. (16)

He who leaves his own teacher, and follows heretical ones, who continuously changes his school,[3] being of a bad disposition, is called a bad Śramaṇa. (17)

He who has left his own house, and busies himself in another's house, who lives by fortune-telling, is called a bad Śramaṇa. (18)

He who eats the food of his relations, and does not like living by alms,[4] who reposes on the seat of the householder, is called a bad Śramaṇa. (19)

Such a monk, who, like the heretics,[5] does not protect himself from sins, who though having the appearance (of a monk) is the lowest among his worthy brethren, is despised in this world like poison; he is nobody in this world and in that beyond. (20)

But he who always avoids these sins, and is pious amongst his brethren, is welcomed in this world like nectar; he conquers this world and the next.[6] (21)

Thus I say.

Eighteenth Lecture: Sañjaya[1]

In the town of Kāmpilya there was a king, named Sañjaya, who possessed numerous troops and war-chariots; once he went a-hunting. (1)

He was surrounded on all sides by a large host of horses, elephants, chariots, and footmen. (2)

He chased the deer on horseback in the Kēsara-park of Kāmpilya; and intent on his sport he killed there the frightened deer. (3)

Now in the Kēsara-park there was a houseless ascetic intent on sacred study and meditating on the Law. (4)

Annihilating sinful inclinations,[2] he meditated in the Asphōta-bower.[3] But the king killed the deer that fled to him. (5)

Now the king on horseback came quickly there; he saw the killed deer and saw the monk there. (6)

The king in his consternation (thought) "I had nearly hurt the monk; ill-fated and cruel me that is mad for the sport." (7)

Having dismissed his horse, the king bowed respectfully to the monk's feet (saying), "Forgive me this, Reverend sir." (8)

But the venerable monk, being plunged in silent meditation, made no reply to the king, who, therefore, was seized with fear. (9)

"I am Sañjaya; answer me, Reverend sir; a monk might by the fire of his wrath reduce millions of men to ashes." (10)

"Be without fear, O king; but grant safety to others also; in this transient world of living beings, why are you addicted to cruelty? (11)

"As you must, of necessity, one day part with everything, in this transient world of living beings, why do you cling to kingly power? (12)

"Transient like a stroke of lightning are life and beauty, which you love so much; you do not comprehend what will benefit you in the next life. (13)

"Wives and children, friends and relations, all are dependent on a man during his life; but they will not follow him in death. (14)

"The sons, in great sorrow, will remove the corpse of their father (to the cemetery); and so will parents do with their sons and relations; O king, do penance! (15)

"O king, other men, glad, and pleased, and well attired, will enjoy the riches (the deceased) had amassed, and will dally with the wives he had so well guarded. (16)

"And whatever actions he has done, good or wicked ones, with their Karman he will depart to his next existence." (17)

Then the king was taught the Law by this monk, and was filled with a great desire for purity, and disregard of worldly objects. (18)

Sañjaya gave up his kingly power and adopted the faith of the Jinas in the presence of the venerable monk Gardabhāli. (19)

A Kṣatriya, who had abandoned his kingdom and had turned monk, said to him: "As you look so happy in outward appearance, you must have peace of mind. (20)

"What is your name, to which Gōtra do you belong, and why have you become an ascetic?[4] How do you venerate the enlightened ones,[5] and how did you come to be called a well-behaved (monk)?" (21)

"My name is Sañjaya; I belong to the Gōtra of Gōtama; my teacher is Gardabhāli, who is conversant with the sacred lore and good conduct. (22)

"O great sage, the man of limited knowledge talks foolishly on these four heads,[6] *viz.* the existence of the soul, its non-existence, idolatry, and the inefficiency of knowledge. (23)

"This has been declared by him who is enlightened, wise, liberated, conversant with the sacred lore and good conduct, who is truthful and of right energy. (24)

"Men who commit sins will go to hell; but those who have walked the road of righteousness, will obtain a place in heaven. (25)

"All this delusive talk (of the heretics) is untrue and without any meaning; I live and walk about according to the rules of self-control. (26)

"I know all these heresies to be contemptible; I know that there will be a life hereafter, and I know my Self. (27)

"I was an illustrious god in the Mahāprāṇa heaven, and reached old age as we here would say of a man who is a hundred years old; but in heaven, hundred years consist of as many Mahāpālīs of Pālīs.[7] (28)

"Descending from the Brahmalōka, I was born as a man. I know exactly the length of my life as well as that of other men. (29)

"A monk should abandon the manifold doctrines (of heretics), and his own fancies, and such deeds as are productive of evil everywhere. One should live up to this wisdom.[8] (30)

"I keep clear of the (superstitious) questions and the spells of laymen, exerting myself day and night (in the true religion). Thinking thus, one should practise austerities. (31)

"And what you of a pure mind asked me just now, that has been revealed by the enlightened one;[9] such knowledge makes part of the creed of the Jinas. (32)

"A wise man believes in the existence of the soul,[10] he avoids the heresy of the non-existence of the soul; possessing true faith one should practise the very difficult Law according to the faith. (33)

"Having learned this pure creed, which is adorned by truth and righteousness, Bharata[11] gave up Bharatavarṣa and all pleasures, and entered the order. (34)

"King Sagara[12] also gave up the ocean-girt Bharatavarṣa and his unrivalled kingly power, and reached perfection through his compassion. (35)

"After having given up Bharatavarṣa, the famous universal monarch of great power, called Maghavan,[13] entered the order. (36)

"King Sanatkumāra,[14] a universal monarch of great power, placed his son on the throne, and then practised austerities. (37)

"Śānti,[15] a universal monarch of great power, the bringer of peace to the world, gave up Bharatavarṣa and reached perfection. (38)

"King Kunthu, the bull of the Aikṣvāka race, the widely famed lord, reached perfection. (39)

"King Ara, after he had given up the sea-girt Bharatavarṣa, reached perfection on becoming exempt from defilement. (40)

"After having given up his large kingdom, his army and war-chariots, his exquisite pleasures, Mahāpadma[16] practised austerities. (41)

"Having brought the (whole) earth under his sceptre, king Hariṣēṇa,[17] who humbled the pride (of other kings), reached perfection. (42)

"Jaya,[18] together with thousands of kings, renouncing the world, practised self-restraint. He reached perfection which has been taught by the Jinas. (43)

"Daśārṇabhadra,[19] giving up his flourishing kingdom of Dasārṇa, turned monk; he renounced the world, being directed to do so by Śakra himself. (44)

"Karakaṇḍu was king of Kaliṅga; Dvimukha, of Pañchāla; Nami, of Vidēha; Naggati (or rather Nagnajit), of Gāndhāra.[20] (45)

"Nami humbled himself, being directed to do so by Sakra himself; the king of Vidēha left the house and became a Śramaṇa. (46)

"These bulls of kings have adopted the faith of the Jinas; after having placed their sons on the throne, they exerted themselves as Śramaṇas. (47)

"Udāyaṇa,[21] the bull of the kings of Sauvīra, renounced the world and turned monk; he entered the order and reached perfection. (48)

"And thus the king of Kāśi,[22] exerting himself for the best truth, abandoned all pleasures, and hewed down, as it were, his Karman like a forest. (49)

"And thus king Vijaya,[23] whose sins were not quite annihilated,[24] turned monk after he, the famous man, had quitted his excellent kingdom. (50)

"And thus the royal seer Mahābala[25] practised severe penance with an undistracted mind, and took upon himself the glory (of self-control). (51)

"Why should a wise man, for bad reasons, live on earth like a madman, since those persons (mentioned above) who reached eminence, exerted themselves strongly? (52)

"I have spoken true words able to promote virtue; some have been saved, some are being saved, and some will be saved. (53)

"Why should a wise man, for bad reasons, bring affliction upon himself? He who has become free from all ties and sins, will reach perfection." (54)

Thus I say.

Nineteenth Lecture: The Son of Mṛgā

In the pleasant town of Sugrīva, which is adorned with parks and gardens, there was the king Balabhadra and Mṛgā, the principal queen. (1)

Their son Balaśrī, also known as Mṛgāputra (*i.e.* son of Mṛgā), the darling of his father and mother, was crown-prince, a (future) lord of ascetics. (2)

In his palace Nandana he dallied with his wives, like the god Dōgundaga,[1] always happy in his mind. (3)

Standing at a window of his palace,[2] the floor of which was inlaid with precious stones and jewels, he looked down on the squares, places, and roads of the town. (4)

Once he saw pass there a restrained Śramaṇa, who practised penance, self-restraint, and self-control, who was full of virtues, and a very mine of good qualities. (5)

Mṛgāputra regarded him with fixed eyes, trying to remember where he had seen the same man before. (6)

While he looked at the saint, and his mind became pure, the remembrance of his former birth carne upon him as he was plunged in doubt. (7)

When the remembrance of his former birth came upon the illustrious Mṛgāputra, he remembered his previous birth and his having been then a Śramaṇa. (8)

Being not delighted with pleasures, but devoted to self-control, he went to his father and mother, and spoke as follows: (9)

"I have learned the five great vows; (I know) the suffering (that awaits the sinner) in hell or in an existence as a brute; I have ceased to take delight in the large ocean (of the Saṃsāra); therefore, O mother, allow me to enter the order. (to)

"O mother, O father, I have enjoyed pleasures which are like poisonous fruit: their consequences are painful, as they entail continuous suffering. (11)

"This body is not permanent, it is impure and of impure origin; it is but a transitory residence (of the soul) and a miserable vessel of suffering. (12)

"I take no delight in this transitory body which one must leave sooner or later, and which is like foam or a bubble. (13)

"And this vain human life, an abode of illness and disease, which is swallowed up by old age and death, does not please me even for a moment. (14)

"Birth is misery, old age is misery, and so are disease and death, and ah, nothing but misery is the Saṃsāra, in which men suffer distress. (15)

"Leaving behind my fields, house, and gold, my son and wife, and my relations, leaving my body needs must, one day, depart. (16)

"As the effect of Kimpāka-fruit[3] is anything but good, so the effect of pleasures enjoyed is anything but good. (17)

"He who starts on a long journey with no provisions, will come to grief on his way there, suffering from hunger and thirst. (18)

"Thus he who without having followed the Law, starts for the next world, will come to grief on his way there, suffering from illness and disease. (19)

"He who starts on a long journey with provisions, will be happy on his way there, not suffering from hunger and thirst. (20)

"Thus he who after having followed the Law, starts for the next world, will be happy on his journey there, being exempt from Karman and suffering. (21)

"As when a house is on fire, the landlord carries away valuable things and leaves behind those of no value; so when the whole world is on fire, as it were, by old age and death, I shall save my Self, if you will permit me." (22, 23)

To him his parents said: "Son, difficult to perform, are the duties of a Śramaṇa; a monk must possess thousands of virtues. (24)

"Impartiality towards all beings in the world, whether friends or enemies, and abstention from injury to living beings throughout the whole life: this is a difficult duty. (25)

"To be never careless in abstaining from falsehood, and to be always careful to speak wholesome truth: this is a difficult duty. (26)

"To abstain from taking of what is not given, even of a toothpick, etc.; and to accept only alms free from faults: this is a difficult duty. (27)

"To abstain from unchastity after one has tasted sensual pleasures, and to keep the severe vow of chastity: this is a very difficult duty. (28)

"To give up all claims on wealth, corn, and servants, to abstain from all undertakings, and not to own anything: this is a very difficult duty. (29)

"Not to eat at night any food of the four kinds,[4] not to put away for later use or to keep a store (of things one wants): this is a very difficult duty. (30)

"Hunger and thirst, heat and cold, molestation by flies and gnats, insults, miserable lodgings, pricking grass, and uncleanliness, blows and threats, corporal punishment and imprisonment, the mendicant's life and fruitless begging: all this is misery. (31, 32)

"Such a life is like that of pigeons (always afraid of dangers); painful is the plucking out of one's hair; difficult is the vow of chastity and hard to keep (even) for a noble man. (33)

"My son, you are accustomed to comfort, you are tender and cleanly;[5] you are not able, my son, to live as a Śramaṇa. (34)

"No repose as long as life lasts; the great burden of duty is heavy like a load of iron, which is difficult to be carried, O son. (35)

"As it is difficult to cross the heavenly Ganges, or to swim against the current, or to swim with one's arms over the sea, so it is difficult to get over the ocean of duties. (36)

"Self-control is untasteful like a mouthful of sand, and to practise penance is as difficult as to walk on the edge of a sword. (37)

"It is difficult (always to observe the rules of) right conduct with one's eyes for ever open like (those of) a snake,[6] O son; it is difficult to eat iron grains, as it were. (38)

"As it is very difficult to swallow burning fire, so is it difficult for a young man to live as a Śramaṇa. (39)

"As it is difficult to fill a bag[7] with wind, so is it difficult for a weak man to live as a Śramaṇa. (40)

"As it is difficult to weigh Mount Mandara in a balance, so it is difficult to live as a Śramaṇa with a steady and fearless mind. (41)

"As it is difficult to swim over the sea with one's arms, so it is difficult for one whose mind is not pacified, (to cross) the ocean of restraint. (42)

"Enjoy the fivefold[8] human pleasures. After you have done enjoying pleasures, O son, you may adopt the Law." (43)

He answered: "O father and mother, it is even thus as you have plainly told; but in this world nothing is difficult for one who is free from desire. (44)

"An infinite number of times have I suffered dreadful pains of body and mind, repeatedly misery and dangers. (45)

"In the Saṃsāra, which is a mine of dangers and a wilderness of old age and death, I have undergone dreadful births and deaths. (46)

"Though fire be hot here, it is infinitely more so there (*viz.* in hell);[9] in hell I have undergone suffering from heat. (47)

"Though there may be cold here, it is of infinitely greater intensity there; in hell I have undergone suffering from cold. (48)

"An infinite number of times have I been roasted over a blazing fire in an oven, screaming loud, head down and feet aloft. (49)

"In the desert which is like a forest on fire, on the Vajravālukā and the Kadambavālukā[10] rivers, I have been roasted an infinite number of times. (50)

"Being suspended upside down over a boiler, shrieking, with no relation to help me, I was cut to pieces with various saws,[11] an infinite number of times. (51)

"I have suffered agonies when I was fastened with fetters on the huge Śālmalī tree, bristling with very sharp thorns, and then pushed up and down. (52)

"An infinite number of times have I been crushed like sugar-cane in presses, shrieking horribly, to atone for my sins, great sinner that I was. (53)

"By black and spotted wild dogs[12] I have, ever so many times, been thrown down, torn to pieces, and lacerated, screaming and writhing. (54)

"When I was born in hell for my sins, I was cut, pierced, and hacked to pieces with swords and daggers, with darts and javelins. (55)

"I have been forcibly yoked to a car of red-hot iron full of fuel,[13] I have been driven on with a goad

and thongs, and have been knocked down like an antelope.[14] (56)

"On piles, in a blazing fire, I have forcibly been burnt and roasted like a buffalo, in atonement for my sins. (57)

"An infinite number of times have I violently been lacerated by birds whose bills were of iron and shaped like tongs, by devilish vultures.[15] (58)

"Suffering from thirst I ran towards the river Vaitaraṇī to drink its water, but in it I was killed (as it were) by blades of razors.[16] (59)

"When suffering from the heat, I went into the forest in which the trees have a foliage of daggers; I have, ever so many times, been cut to pieces by the dropping dagger-leaves. (60)

"An infinite number of times have I suffered hopelessly from mallets and knives, forks and maces, which broke my limbs. (61)

"Ever so many times have I been slit, cut, mangled, and skinned with keen-edged razors, knives, and shears. (62)

"As[17] an antelope I have, against my will, been caught, bound, and fastened in snares and traps, and frequently I have been killed. (63)

"As a fish I have, against my will, been caught with hooks and in bow-nets; I have therein been scraped, slit, and killed, an infinite number of times. (64)

"As a bird I have been caught by hawks, trapped in nets, and bound with bird-lime, and I have been killed, an infinite number of times. (65)

"As a tree I have been felled, slit, sawn into planks, and stripped of the bark by carpenters with axes,[18] hatchets, etc., an infinite number of times. (66)

"As iron I have been malleated, cut, torn, and filed by blacksmiths,[19] an infinite number of times. (67)

"I have been made to drink hissing molten copper, iron, tin, and lead under horrid shrieks, an infinite number of times. (68)

"You like meat minced or roasted; I have been made to eat, ever so many times, poisoned meat, and red-hot to boot. (69)

"You like wine, liquor, spirits, and honey;[20] I have been made to drink burning fat and blood. (70)

"Always frightened, trembling, distressed, and suffering, I have experienced the most exquisite pain and misery. (71)

"I have experienced in hell sharp, acute and severe, horrible, intolerable, dreadful, and formidable pain. (72)

"O father, infinitely more painful is the suffering in hell than any suffering in the world of men. (73)

"In every kind of existence I have undergone suffering which was not interrupted by a moment's reprieve." (74)

To him his parents said: "Son, a man is free to enter the order, but it causes misery to a Śramaṇa that he may not remedy any ailings." (75)

He answered: "O father and mother, it is even thus as you have plainly told; but who takes care of beasts and birds in the woods? (76)

"As a wild animal[21] by itself roams about in the woods, thus I shall practise the Law by controlling myself and doing penance. (77)

"When in a large forest a wild animal falls very sick at the foot of a tree, who is there to cure it? (78)

"Or who will give it medicine? or who will inquire after its health? or who will get food and drink for it, and feed it? (79)

"When it is in perfect health, it will roam about in woods and on (the shores of) lakes in search of food and drink. (80)

"When it has eaten and drunk in woods and lakes, it will walk about and go to rest according to the habits of wild animals. (81)

"In the same way a pious monk goes to many places and walks about just as the animals, but afterwards he goes to the upper regions. (82)

"As a wild animal goes by itself to many places, lives in many places, and always gets its food; thus a monk on his begging-tour should not despise nor blame (the food he gets). (83)

"I shall imitate this life of animals." "Well, my son, as you please." With his parents' permission he gave up all his property. (84)

"I shall imitate this life of animals, which makes one free from all misery, if you will permit me." "Go, my son, as you please." (85)

When he had thus made his parents repeat their permission, he gave up for ever his claims in any property, just as the snake casts off its slough. (86)

His power and wealth, his friends, wives, sons, and relations he gave up as if he shook off the dust from his feet, and then he went forth. (87)

He observed the five great vows, practised the five Samitis, and was protected by the three Guptis;[22] he exerted himself to do mental as well as bodily penance. (88)

He was without property, without egoism, without attachment, without conceit,[23] impartial towards all beings, whether they move or not. (89)

He was indifferent to success or failure (in begging), to happiness and misery, to life and death, to blame and praise, to honour and insult. (90)

He turned away from conceit and passions, from injurious, hurtful, and dangerous actions,[24] from gaiety and sadness; he was free from sins and fetters. (91)

He had no interest in this world and no interest in the next world; he was indifferent to unpleasant and pleasant things,[25] to eating and fasting. (92)

He prevented the influx of Karman (āsrava) through all bad channels;[26] by meditating upon himself he obtained praiseworthy self-purification and sacred knowledge. (93)

Thus he thoroughly purified himself by knowledge, right conduct, faith, penance, and pure meditations, and after having lived many years as a Śramaṇa, he reached perfection after breaking his fast once only every month. (94, 95)

Thus act the enlightened ones, the learned, the clever; like Mṛgāputra they turn away from pleasures. (96)

When you have heard the words of the illustrious and famous son of Mṛgā, his perfect practise of austerities, and his liberation, famous in the three worlds, you will despise wealth, the cause of misery, and the fetter of egoism, the cause of many dangers, and you will bear the excellent and pleasant yoke of the Law that leads to the great happiness of Nirvāṇa. (97, 98)

Thus I say.

Twentieth Lecture: The Great Duty of the Nirgranthas

Piously adoring the perfected and the restrained saints, listen to my true instruction which (teaches the real) profit (of men), religion, and liberation.[1] (1)

King Śrēṇika,[2] the ruler of Magadha, who possessed many precious things, once made a pleasure-excursion to the Maṇḍikukṣi Chaitya.[3] (2)

It was a park like Nandana,[4] with trees and creepers of many kinds, peopled by various birds, and full of various flowers. (3)

There he saw a restrained and concentrated saint sitting below a tree, who looked delicate and accustomed to comfort. (4)

When the king saw his figure, his astonishment at that ascetic's figure was very great and unequalled. (5)

"O his colour, O his figure, O the loveliness of the noble man, O his tranquillity, O his perfection, O his disregard for pleasures!" (6)

Adoring his feet and keeping him on his right side (he sat down), neither too far off nor too close by, and asked him with his hands clasped: (7)

"Though a young nobleman, you have entered the order; in an age fit for pleasure you exert yourself as a Śramaṇa, O ascetic; I want to hear you explain this." (8)

"I am without a protector, O great king; there is nobody to protect me, I know no friend nor any one to have sympathy with me." (9)

Then king Śrēṇika, the ruler of Magadha, laughed: "How should there be nobody to protect one so accomplished as you?" (10)

"I am the protector of religious men;[5] O monk; enjoy pleasures together with your friends and relations; for it is a rare chance to be born as a human being." (11)

"You yourself are without a protector, Śrēṇika, ruler of Magadha; and as you are without a protector, how can you protect anybody else?" (12)

When the saint had addressed this unprecedented speech to the king, who was greatly moved and astonished, and struck with astonishment, (he answered):[6] (13)

"I have horses, elephants, and subjects, a town and a seraglio, power and command: enjoy human pleasures. (14)

"In possession of so great means, which permit the owner to enjoy all pleasures, how could he be without protection? Reverend sir, you speak untruth." (15)

"O king, you do not know the meaning and origin[7] of (the word) "without protection," nor how one comes to be without protection or with protection, O ruler of men. (16)

"Hear, O great king, with an undistracted mind in what way a man can be said to be "without protection," and with what purpose I have said all this. (17)

"There is a town Kauśāmbī by name, which is among towns what Indra[8] is (among the gods); there lived my father, who possessed great wealth. (18)

"In my childhood, O great king, I caught a very bad eye-disease and a severe burning fever in all my limbs, O ruler of men. (19)

"My eyes ached as if a cruel enemy thrust a sharp tool in the hollow of my body. (20)

"In the back, the heart,[9] and the head, I suffered dreadful and very keen pains equal to a stroke of lightning. (21)

"Then the best physicians came to my help, who cure by their medical art and by spells, who were versed in their science, and well knew spells and roots. (22)

"They tried to cure me according to the fourfold science[10] which they had been taught; but they could not rid me of my pains: hence I say that I am without protection. (23)

"My father would have spent all he possessed, for my sake; but he could not rid me of my pains, hence I say that I am without protection. (24)

"My mother, O great king, was agonized with grief about her son; but she could not, etc. (25)

"O great king, my own brothers, the elder and younger ones, could not rid me of my pains, etc. (26)

"O great king, my own sisters, the elder and younger ones, could not, etc. (27)

"O great king, my loving and faithful wife moistened my breast with the tears of her eyes. (28)

"The poor lady did not eat, nor drink, nor bathe, nor use perfumes, wreaths, and anointment, with my knowledge or without it. (29)

"O great king, she did not leave[11] my side even for a moment; but she could not rid me of my pains, hence I say that I am without protection. (30)

"Then I said: It is very hard to bear pains again and again in the endless Circle of Births. (31)

"If I, for once, shall get rid of these great pains, I shall become a houseless monk, calm, restrained, and ceasing to act. (32)

"While I thought so, I fell asleep, O ruler of men; and after that night my pains had vanished. (33)

"Then in the morning of the next day I took leave of my relations and became a houseless monk, calm, restrained, and ceasing to act. (34)

"Thus I became the protector of myself and of others besides, of all living beings, whether they move or not. (35)

"My own Self is the river Vaitaraṇī, my own Self the Śālmalī tree;[12] my own Self is the miraculous cow Kāmaduh, my own Self the park Nandana. (36)

"My own Self is the doer and undoer of misery and happiness; my own Self, friend and foe, according as I act well or badly. (37)

"But there is still another want of protection, O king; hear, therefore, O king, attentively with concentrated thoughts, how some easily discouraged men go astray after having adopted the Law of the Nirgranthas.[13] (38)

"If an ordained monk, through carelessness, does not strictly keep the great vows, if he does not restrain himself, but desires pleasure, then his fetters will not be completely cut off. (39)

"One who does not pay constant attention to his walking, his speaking, his begging, his receiving and keeping (of things necessary for a monk), and his easing nature,[14] does not follow the road trod by the Lord. (40)

"One who for a long time wears a shaven crown and mortifies himself, but who is careless with regard to the vows, and neglects penance and self-control, will not be a winner in the battle (of life). (41)

"He is empty like a clenched[15] fist, (of no value) like an uncoined[16] false Kārṣāpaṇa or like a piece of glass resembling turquoise, he is held lightly by men of discernment. (42)

"He who has the character of a sinner, though he lays great stress on the outward signs of his calling[17] as a means of living; he who does not control himself, though he pretends to do so; will come to grief for a long time. (43)

"As the poison Kālakūṭa kills him who drinks it; as a weapon cuts him who awkwardly handles it; as a Vētāla kills him who does not lay him; so the Law harms him who mixes it up with sensuality. (44)

"He who practises divination from bodily marks and dreams, who is well versed in augury and superstitious rites, who gains a sinful living by practising magic tricks,[18] will have no refuge at the time (of retribution). (45)

"The sinner, always wretched, goes from darkness to darkness, to utter misery; the unholy man who breaks the rules of monks, rushes, as it were, to hell, and to be born again as a brute. (46)

"He who accepts forbidden alms, *viz.* such food as he himself asks for, as has been bought for his sake, or as he gets regularly (as by right and custom), who like fire devours everything, will go to hell from here, after having sinned. (47)

"A cut-throat enemy will not do him such harm as his own perversity will do him; the man without pity will feel repentance in the hour of death. (48)

"In vain he adopts nakedness, who errs about matters of paramount interest; neither this world nor the next will be his; he is a loser in both respects in the world. (49)

"Thus the self-willed sinner who leaves the road of the highest Jinas, who with the appetite of an osprey is desirous of pleasure, will grieve in useless sorrow. (50)

"A wise man who hears this discourse, an instruction full of precious wisdom, and who deserts every path of the wicked, should walk the road of the great Nirgranthas. (51)

"He who possesses virtuous conduct and life, who has practised the best self-control, who keeps from sinful influences,[19] and who has destroyed his Karman, will reach (in the end) the greatest, best, and permanent place (*viz.* mukti)," (52)

Thus the austere and calm, great ascetic and great sage who kept great vows and possessed great fame, preached at great length this great sermon: the great duty of the Nirgranthas. (53)

And king Śrēṇika, pleased, spoke thus: "You have truly shown what it is to be without protection. (54)

"You have made the best use of human birth, you have made a true gain, O great sage, you are a protector (of mankind at large) and of your relations, for you have entered the path of the best Jinas. (55)

"You are the protector of all unprotected beings, O ascetic; I ask you to forgive me: I desire you to put me right. (56)

"That by asking you I have disturbed your meditation, and that I invited you to enjoy pleasures, all this you must forgive me." (57)

When the lion of kings had thus, with the greatest devotion, praised the lion of houseless monks, he, together with his wives, servants, and relations, became a staunch believer in the Law, with a pure mind. (58)

The ruler of men, with the hair on his body joyfully erected, bowed his head (to the monk), keeping him on his right side, and departed. (59)

And the other, rich in virtues, protected by the three Guptis, and abstaining from injuring (living beings) in the three ways (*viz.* by thought, words, and acts), travelled about on the earth, free like a bird, and exempt from delusion. (60)

Thus I say.

Twenty-First Lecture: Samudrapāla

In Champā there lived a Śrāvaka, the merchant Pālita, who was a disciple of the noble and venerable Mahāvīra. (1)

As a Śrāvaka he was well versed in the doctrines of the Nirgranthas. Once he went by boat to the town of Pihuṇḍa on business. (2)

A merchant gave him his daughter while he was doing business in Pihuṇḍa. When she was big with child, he took her with him on his returning home. (3)

Now the wife of Pālita was delivered of a child at sea; as the boy was born at sea (samudra), he was named Samudrapāla. (4)

Our merchant, the Śrāvaka, went leisurely to Kampā, to his house; in his house the boy grew up surrounded by comfort. (5)

He studied the seventy-two arts, and acquired knowledge of the world;[1] he was in the bloom of youth, and had a fine figure and good looks. (6)

His father procured him a beautiful wife, Rūpiṇī, with whom he amused himself in his pleasant palace, like a Dōgundaga god.[2] (7)

Once upon a time he saw from the window of his palace a man sentenced to death, dressed for execution, on his way to the place of execution. (8)

Agitated by what he saw, Samudrapāla spoke thus: "Of wicked actions this is the bad result." (9)

He became enlightened at once, the venerable man, and he was immensely agitated; he took leave of his parents, and entered the state of houselessness. (10)

Abandoning the great distress to which the worldly[3] are liable, the great delusion, and whatever causes fear, one should adopt the Law of monks,[4] the vows, the virtues, and the (endurance of) calamities. (11)

One should keep the five great vows, *viz.* not to kill, to speak the truth, not to steal, to be chaste, to have no property whatever; a wise man should follow the Law taught by the Jinas. (12)

A monk should have compassion on all beings, should be of a forbearing character, should be restrained and chaste, and abstaining from everything sinful; he should live with his senses under control. (13)

Now and then[5] he should travel in one country, taking into consideration its resources and his own ability; like a lion he should not be frightened by any noise; and whatever words he hears, he should not make an improper reply. (14)

In utter indifference he should walk about, and bear everything, be it pleasant or unpleasant; he should not approve of everything everywhere, nor care for[6] respectful treatment or blame. (15)

There are many opinions here among men, which a monk places in their true light; there will rise many dangerous and dreadful calamities, caused by gods, men, or animals, which are difficult to be borne and cause easily-discouraged men to sink under them; but a monk who comes in contact with them will not be afraid, like a stately elephant at the head of the battle. (16, 17)

Cold and heat, flies and gnats, unpleasant feelings, and many diseases attack the body; without flinching[7] he should bear them, and should not recall to his memory the pleasures he once enjoyed. (18)

Giving up love, hatred, and delusion, a monk who is always careful and who is steadfast even as Mount Mēru cannot be shaken by the storm, should bear calamities, guarding himself. (19)

A great sage should be neither too elevated by pride nor too humble, he should not care for respectful treatment nor blame; an ascetic who has ceased (to act), will by means of his simplicity enter the path of Nirvāṇa. (20)

He is neither grieved nor pleased (by anything),[8] he abandons his relations with men, he ceases (to act), is intent on the benefit of his soul, he strives for the highest good (*viz.* mukti), and uses the means to reach it, free from sorrow, egoism, and any kind of property. (21)

A merciful (monk) should use beds distant from others, which are not got ready for his sake[9] nor strewn (with leaves or things considered to be possessed of life); he should sustain such hardships as the sages are accustomed to. (22)

The great sage (Samudrapāla), understanding the sacred lore and practising completely the best Law, shone forth like the sun in the sky, being possessed of the highest knowledge and glory. (23)

Having annihilated his Karman both meritorious and sinful, being steadfast,[10] and free from all fetters, Samudrapāla crossed the ocean-like Flood of worldly existence and obtained exemption from transmigration. (24)

Thus I say.

Twenty-Second Lecture: Rathanēmi

In the town of Śauryapura[1] there was a powerful king, Vasudēva by name, who possessed the characteristic marks of a king. (1)

He had two wives, Rōhiṇī and Dēvakī; each of them had a beloved son, Rāma and Kēśava. (2)

In the town of Śauryapura there was (another) powerful king, Samudravijaya by name, who possessed the characteristic marks of a king. (3)

His wife was Śivā by name; and her famous son was the venerable Ariṣṭanēmi, the saviour of the world and the lord of ascetics. (4)

This Ariṣṭanēmi, who was gifted with an excellent voice and possessed the thousand and eight lucky marks of the body, was a Gautama, and his skin was black. (5)

His body was strong like that of a bull, and hard like steel; he was well proportioned, and had a belly like that of a fish.

Kēśava asked the girl Rājīmatī[2] in marriage for him. (6)

Now this daughter of an excellent king[3] was virtuous and well looking; she possessed all lucky marks of the body, and shone forth like the lightning Saudāmanī. (7)

Her father said to the powerful Vāsudēva: "Let the prince come here that I may give him my daughter." (8)

He had taken a bath containing all (lucky) herbs, and had performed the customary ceremonies; he wore a suit of heavenly clothes and was decked out with ornaments. (9)

Riding on the best mast elephant[4] of Vāsudēva he looked beautiful, like a jewel worn on the head. (10)

He sat under a raised umbrella, fanned by two chowries, and he was surrounded on all sides by a host of Daśārhas[5] and by a complete army drawn up in rank and file, while the heavenly sound of musical instruments reached the sky. (11, 12)

With such pomp and splendour the hero of the Vṛṣṇis started from his own palace. (13)

On his way he saw animals, kept in cages and enclosures, overcome by fear and looking miserable. (14)

Seeing them on the point of being killed for the sake of their flesh, and to be eaten afterwards, the great sage spoke to his charioteer[6] thus: (15)

"Why are[7] all these animals, which desire to be happy, kept in cages and enclosures?" (16)

Then the charioteer answered: "Lucky are these animals because at thy wedding they will furnish food for many people." (17)

Having heard these words, which announced the slaughter of many animals, the great sage, full of compassion and kindness to living beings, meditated thus: (18)

"If for my sake many living beings are killed, I shall not obtain happiness in the next world." (19)

Then the famous man presented the charioteer with his pair of earrings, his neck-chain, and all his ornaments. (20)

When he had formed his resolution, the gods descended (from heaven), according to the established custom, to celebrate, with great pomp together with their retinue, the event of his renunciation. (21)

Surrounded by gods and men, and sitting on an excellent palankin, the Venerable One left Dvārakā and ascended mount Raivataka.[8] (22)

On arriving at the park he descended from his excellent palankin, surrounded by a crowd of thousands, and then his renunciation took place, while the moon was in conjunction with Chitrā.[9] (23)

Then he himself plucked out his delightfully-perfumed, soft, and curled hair in five handfuls. (24)

And Vāsudēva said to that subduer of the senses, who had plucked out his hair: "O lord of ascetics, may you soon obtain what you wish and desire. (25)

"Increase in knowledge, faith, and right conduct, in forbearance and perfection!" (26)

In this manner Rāma and Kēsava, the Daśārhas, and many people paid homage to Ariṣṭanēmi and then returned to the town of Dvārakā. (27)

When the daughter of the king heard of the ordination of the Jina, laughter and gaiety forsook her, and she was overwhelmed with affliction.[10] (28)

Rājīmatī thought: "Shame upon my life, that I have been forsaken by him! it is better I should turn nun." (29)

Firm and decided she cut off her tresses which were black like bees and dressed with a brush and comb.[11] (30)

And Vāsudēva said to her who had cut off her hair, and subdued her senses: "Lady, cross the dreadful ocean of the Saṃsāra without difficulty!" (31)

When she had entered the order, the virtuous and very learned lady induced there many people, her relations and servants, to enter the order too. (32)

On her way to mount Raivataka it began to rain; her clothes being wet, she entered a cave and waited there in the darkness while it was raining. (33)

She took off her clothes and was naked as she was born, thus she was seen by Rathanēmi,[12] whose (peace of) mind (thereby) disturbed; and afterwards she saw him. (34)

She was frightened when she discovered herself alone with the monk; folding her arms over her breast she sank down trembling. (35)

When the prince, Samudravijaya's son, saw her frightened and trembling, he spoke the following words: (36)

"I am Rathanēmi, O dear, beautiful, sweetly-speaking lady! Do accept me for your lover, O slender one,[13] you shall have no cause to complain. (37)

"Come, let us enjoy pleasures, for it is a rare chance to be born a human being; after we have enjoyed pleasures, we shall enter on the path of the Jinas." (38)

When Rājīmatī perceived that Rathanēmi's strength of will was broken, and temptation had got the better of him, she did not lose her presence of mind and defended her Self on that occasion. (39)

The daughter of the best king, true to self-control and her vows, maintained the honour of her clan and family, and her virtue, and spoke to him: (40)

"If you owned the beauty of Vaiśramaṇa,[14] the pleasing manners of Nalakūbara,[15] if you were like Purandara[16] himself, I should have no desire for you. (41)

"Fie upon you, famous knight, who want to quaff the vomited drink for the sake of this life; it would be better for you to die.[17] (42)

"I am the daughter of the Bhōga-king,[18] and you are an Andhakavṛṣṇi; being born in a noble family let us not become like Gandhana-snakes;[19] firmly practise self-control! (43)

"If you fall in love with every woman you see, you will be without hold like the Haṭha-plant,[20] driven before the wind. (44)

"As a herdsman or a keeper of goods does not own the things (he has the care of), so you will not truly own Śramaṇahood." (45)

Having heard these well-spoken words of the virtuous lady, he returned to the Law like an elephant driven by the hook.[21] (46)

Protected in thoughts, words, and acts, subduing his senses and keeping the vows, he practised true Śramaṇahood throughout life. (47)

After practising severe austerities both of them became Kēvalins, and having completely annihilated their Karman, they reached the highest perfection. (48)

Thus act the enlightened, the wise, the clever ones; they turn from pleasures as did this best of men.[22] (49)

Thus I say.

Twenty-Third Lecture:[1] Kēsi and Gautama

There was a Jina, Pārśva[2] by name, an Arhat, worshipped by the people, who was thoroughly enlightened and omniscient, a prophet of the Law, and a Jina. (1)

And there was a famous disciple of this Light of the World, the young Śramaṇa Kēśi, who had completely mastered the sciences and right conduct. (2)

He possessed the light of Śruta and Avadhi knowledge,[3] and was surrounded by a crowd of disciples; wandering from village to village he arrived in the town of Śrāvastī. (3)

In the district of that town there is a park, called Tinduka; there he took up his abode in a pure place to live and sleep in. (4)

Now at that time there lived the Prophet of the Law, the Jina, who in the whole world is known as the venerable Vardhamāna. (5)

And there was a famous disciple of this Light of the World, the venerable Gautama by name, who had completely mastered the sciences and right conduct. (6)

He knew the twelve Angās, was enlightened, and was surrounded by a crowd of disciples; wandering from village to village he too arrived in Śrāvastī. (7)

In the district of that town there is a park Kōṣṭhaka; there he took up his abode in a pure place to live and sleep in. (8)

The young Śramaṇa Kēśi and the famous Gautama, both lived there, protecting themselves (by the Guptis) and being careful. (9)

The pupils of both, who, controlled themselves, who practised austerities, who possessed virtues, and who protected their Self, made the following reflection: (10)

"Is our Law the right one, or is the other Law[4] the right one? are our conduct and doctrines right, or the other? (it)

"The Law as taught by the great sage Pārśva, which recognises but four vows,[5] or the Law taught by Vardhamāna, which enjoins five vows? (12)

"The Law which forbids clothes (for a monk), or that which (allows) an under and upper garment? Both pursuing the same end, what has caused their difference?" (13)

Knowing the thoughts of their pupils, both Kēśi and Gautama made up their minds to meet each other. (14)

Gautama, knowing what is proper and what is due to the older section (of the church), went to the Tinduka park, accompanied by the crowd, his pupils. (15)

When Kēśi, the young monk, saw Gautama approach, he received him with all becoming attention. (16)

He at once offered Gautama the four pure kinds of straw and hay[6] to sit upon. (17)

Kēśi, the young Śramaṇa, and the famous Gautama, sitting together, shone forth with a lustre like that of sun and moon. (18)

There assembled many heretics out of curiosity, and many thousands of laymen; (19)

Gods, Dānavas, Gandharvas, Yakṣas, Rākṣasas, and Kinnaras (assembled there), and there came together invisible ghosts[7] too. (20)

Kēśi said to Gautama, "I want to ask you something, holy man." Then to these words of Kēśi Gautama made the following reply: "Sir, ask whatever you like." Then with his permission Kēśi spoke to Gautama: (21, 22)

"The Law taught by the great sage Pārśva, recognises but four vows, whilst that of Vardhamāna enjoins five. (23)

"Both Laws pursuing the same end, what has caused this difference? Have you no misgivings about this twofold Law, O wise man?" (24)

Then to these words of Kēśi Gautama made the following reply:

"Wisdom recognises the truth of the Law and the ascertainment of true things. (25)

"The first[8] saints were simple but slow of understanding, the last saints prevaricating and slow of understanding, those between the two simple and wise; hence there are two forms of the Law.[9] (26)

"The first could but with difficulty understand the precepts of the Law, and the last could only with difficulty observe them, but those between them easily understood and observed them." (27)

"Well, Gautama, you possess wisdom, you have destroyed my doubt; but I have another doubt which you must explain to me, Gautama. (28)

"The Law taught by Vardhamāna forbids clothes, but that of the great sage Pārśva allows an under and upper garment. (29)

"Both Laws pursuing the same end, what has caused this difference? Have you no misgivings about this twofold Law, O wise man?" (30)

To these words of Kēśi Gautama made the following reply: "Deciding the matter by their superior knowledge, (the Tīrthakaras) have fixed what is necessary for carrying out the Law. (31)

"The various outward marks (of religious men) have been introduced in order that people might recognise them as such; the reason for the characteristic marks is their usefulness for religious life and their distinguishing character. (32)

"Now the opinion (of the Tīrthakaras) is that knowledge, faith. and right conduct are the true causes of final liberation, (and not the outward marks)." (33)

"Well, Gautama, you possess wisdom, you have destroyed my doubt; but I have another doubt, which you must explain to me, Gautama. (34)

"Gautama, you stand in the midst of many thousand (foes) who make an attack on you; how have you vanquished them?[10] (35)

"By vanquishing one, five are vanquished; by vanquishing five, ten are vanquished; by this tenfold victory, I vanquish all foes." (36)

Kēśi said to Gautama: "Whom do you call a foe?" To these words of Kēśi Gautama made the following reply: (37)

"Self is the one invincible foe, (together with the four) cardinal passions,[11] (*viz.* anger, pride, deceit, and greed, they are five) and the (five) senses (make ten). These (foes), O great sage, I have regularly vanquished." (38)

"Well, Gautama, etc. (as in verse 28). (19)

"We see many beings in this world who are bound by fetters; how have you got rid of your fetters and are set free, O sage?" (40)

"Having cut off all fetters, and having destroyed them by the right means, I have got rid of my fetters and am set free, O sage." (41)

Kēśi said to Gautama: "What do you call fetters?"

To these words of Kēśi Gautama made the following reply: (42)

"Love, hatred, etc., are heavy fetters, attachment is a dangerous one; having regularly destroyed them, I live up to the rules of conduct." (43)

"Well, Gautama, etc. (as in verse 28). (44)

"O Gautama, in the innermost heart there grows a plant which brings forth poisonous fruit; how have you torn it out?" (45)

"I have thoroughly clipped that plant, and torn it out altogether with its roots; thus I have got rid of the poisonous fruit." (46)

Kēśi said to Gautama, "What do you call that plant?" To these words of Kēśi Gautama made the following reply: (47)

"Love of existence is that dreadful plant which brings forth dreadful fruit; having regularly torn it out, I live pleasantly." (48)

"Well, Gautama, etc. (as in verse 28). (49)

"Gautama, there is blazing up a frightful fire which burns[12] the embodied beings; how have you put it out?" (50)

"Taking water, excellent water, from (the river) produced by the great cloud, I always pour it over my body; thus sprinkled the fire does not burn me." (51)

Kēśi said to Gautama, "What do you call the fire?" To these words of Kēśi Gautama made the following reply: (52)

"The passions are the fire; knowledge, a virtuous life, and penances are the water; sprinkled with the drops of knowledge the fire of the passions is extinguished and does not burn me." (53)

"Well, Gautama, etc. (as in verse 28). (54)

"The unruly, dreadful, bad horse, on which you sit, runs about, Gautama! how comes it to pass that it does not run off with you?" (55)

"I govern it well in its course by the bridle of knowledge; it does not go astray with me, it keeps to the right path." (56)

Kēśi said to Gautama, "What do you call this horse?" To these words of Kēśi Gautama made the following reply: (57)

"The mind is that unruly, dreadful, bad horse; I govern it by the discipline of the Law (so that it becomes a well-) trained Kambōja-steed."[13] (58)

"Well, Gautama, etc. (as in verse 28). (59)

"There are many bad roads in this world, which lead men astray; how do you avoid, Gautama, going astray as you are on the road?" (60)

"They all are known to me, those who are in the right path and those who have chosen a wrong path; therefore I do not go astray, O sage!" (61)

Kēśi said to Gautama, "What do you call the path?" To these words of Kēśi Gautama made the following reply: (62)

"The heterodox and the heretics have all chosen a wrong path; the right path is that taught by the Jinas; it is the most excellent path." (63)

"Well, Gautama, etc. (as in verse 28). (64)

"Is there a shelter, a refuge, a firm ground for the beings carried away by the great flood of water? do you know the island, O Gautama?" (65)

"There is a large, great island in the midst of water, which is not inundated by the great flood of water." (66)

Kēśi said to Gautama, "What do you call this island?" To these words of Kēśi Gautama made the following reply: (67)

"The flood is old age and death, which carry away living beings; Law is the island, the firm ground, the refuge, the most excellent shelter." (68)

"Well, Gautama, etc. (as in verse 28). (69)

"On the ocean with its many currents there drifts a boat; how will you, Gautama, on board of it reach the opposite shore?" (70)

"A boat that leaks will not reach the opposite shore; but a boat that does not leak, will reach it." (71)

Kēśi said to Gautama, "What do you call this boat?" To these words of Kēśi Gautama made the following reply: (72)

"The body is the boat, life is the sailor, and the Circle of Births is the ocean which is crossed by the great sages." (73)

"Well, Gautama, etc. (as in verse 28). (74)

"In this dreadfully dark gloom there live many beings; who will bring light into the whole world of living beings?" (75)

"The spotless sun has risen which illuminates the whole world; he will bring light into the whole world of living beings." (76)

Kēśi said to Gautama, "What do you call this sun?" To these words of Kēśi Gautama made the following reply: (77)

"Risen has he who put an end to the Circle of Births, the omniscient Jina, the luminary, who brings light into the whole world of living beings." (78)

"Well, Gautama, etc. (as in verse 28). (79)

"Do you, O sage, know a safe, happy, and quiet place for living beings which suffer from pains[14] of body and mind?" (80)

"There is a safe place in view of all, but difficult of approach, where there is no old age nor death, no pain nor disease." (81)

Kēśi said to Gautama, "What is this place called?" To these words of Kēśi Gautama made the following reply: (82)

"It is what is called Nirvāṇa, or freedom from pain, or perfection, which is in view of all; it is the safe, happy, and quiet place which the great sages reach. (83)

"That is the eternal place, in view of all, but difficult of approach. Those sages who reach it are free from sorrows, they have put an end to the stream of existence." (84)

"Well, Gautama, you possess wisdom, you have destroyed my doubt; obeisance to you, who are not troubled by doubts, who are the ocean, as it were, of all Sūtras." (85)

After his doubt had been solved, Kēśi, of enormous sanctity, bowed his head to the famous Gautama. (86)

And in the pleasant (Tinduka park) he sincerely adopted the Law of the five vows, which was proclaimed by the first Tīrthakara, according to the teaching of the last Tīrthakara. (87)

In that meeting of Kēśi and Gautama, knowledge and virtuous conduct were for ever brought to eminence, and subjects of the greatest importance were settled. (88)

The whole assembly was greatly pleased and fixed their thoughts on the right way. They praised Kēśi and Gautama: "May the venerable ones show us favour!" (89)

Thus I say.

Twenty-Fourth Lecture: The Samitis

The eight articles[1] of the creed are the Samitis and the Guptis; there are five Samitis and three Guptis. (1)

The Samitis[2] are: 1. īryā-samiti (going by paths trodden by men, beasts, carts, etc., and looking carefully so as not to occasion the death of any living creature); 2. bhāṣā-samiti (gentle, salutary, sweet, righteous speech); 3. ēṣaṇā-samiti (receiving alms in a manner to avoid the forty-two faults that are laid down); 4. ādāna-samiti (receiving and keeping of the things necessary for religious exercises, after having carefully examined them); 5. uccāra-samiti (performing the operations of nature in an unfrequented place). The three Guptis (which are here included in the term Samiti in its wider application) are: 1. mano-gupti (preventing the mind from wandering in the forest of sensual pleasures by employing it in contemplation, study, etc.); 2. vāg-gupti (preventing the tongue from saying bad things by a vow of silence, etc.); 3. kāya-gupti (putting the body in an immovable posture as in the case of Kāyōtsarga). (2)

The eight Samitis are thus briefly enumerated, in which the whole creed taught by the Jinas and set forth in the twelve Angās, is comprehended. (3)

1. The walking of a well-disciplined monk should be pure in four respects: in respect to 1. the cause;[3] 2. the time; 3. the road; 4. the effort.[4] (4)

The cause is: knowledge, faith, and right conduct; the time is day-time; the road excludes bad ways. (5)

The effort is fourfold, *viz.* as regards: 1. substance, 2. place, 3. time, and 4. condition of mind. Hear me explain them. (6)

With regard to substance: the (walking monk) should look with his eyes; with regard to place: the space of a yuga (*i.e.* four hastas or cubits); with regard to time: as long as he walks; and with regard to condition of mind: carefully.[5] (7)

He walks carefully who pays attention only to his walk and his body (executing it), whilst he avoids attending to the objects of sense, but (minds) his study, the latter in all five ways.[6] (8)

2. To give way to: anger, pride, deceit and greed, laughter, fear, loquacity and slander;[7] these eight faults should a well-disciplined monk avoid; he should use blameless and concise speech at the proper time. (9, 10)

3. As regards begging,[8] a monk should avoid the faults in the search,[9] in the receiving,[10] and in the use[11] of the three kinds of objects, *viz.* food, articles of use, and lodging. (11)

A zealous monk should avoid in the first (*i.e.* in the search for alms) the faults occasioned either by the giver (udgama) or by the receiver (utpādana); in the second (*i.e.* in the receiving of alms) the faults inherent in the receiving; and in the use of the articles received, the four faults.[12] (12)

4. If a monk takes up or lays down the two kinds of things belonging to his general and supplementary[13] outfit, he should proceed in the following way. (13)

A zealous monk should wipe the thing after having inspected it with his eyes, and then he should take it up or put it down, having the Samiti in both respects.[14] (14)

5. Excrements, urine, saliva, mucus, uncleanliness of the body, offals of food, waste things, his own body (when he is about to die), and everything of this description (is to be disposed of in the way to be described). (15)

[A place may be not frequented and not seen (by people), or not frequented but seen, or frequented and not seen, or frequented and seen. (16)][15]

In a place neither frequented nor seen by other people, which offers no obstacles to self-control, which is even, not covered with grass or leaves[16], and has been brought into its present condition[17] not long ago, which is spacious, has an inanimate surface-layer,[18] not too near (the village, etc.), not perforated by holes, and is exempt from insects and seeds—in such a place he should leave his excrements, etc. (17, 18)

The five Samitis are thus briefly enumerated, I shall now explain in due order the three Guptis.[19] (19)

1. There is, 1. truth; 2. untruth; 3. a mixture of truth and untruth; 4. a mixture of what is not true, and what is not untrue. The Gupti of mind refers to all four.[20] (20)

A zealous monk should prevent his mind from desires for the misfortune of somebody else,[21] from thoughts on acts which cause misery to living beings,[22] and from thoughts on acts which cause their destruction.[23] (21)

2. The Gupti of speech is also of four kinds (referring to the four divisions as in verse 20). (22)

A zealous monk should prevent his speech from (expressing) desires, etc. (as in verse 21). (23)

3. In standing, sitting, lying down, jumping, going, and in the use of his organs, a zealous monk should prevent his body from intimating obnoxious desires, from doing acts which cause misery to living beings, or which cause their destruction. (24, 25)

These are the five Samitis for the practice of the religious life, and the Guptis for the prevention of everything sinful. (26)

This is the essence of the creed, which a sage should thoroughly put into practice; such a wise man will soon get beyond the Circle of Births. (27)

Thus I say.

Twenty-Fifth Lecture: The True Sacrifice

There was a famous Brāhmaṇa, Jayaghōṣa by name, who was born in a Brāhmanical family, but who was pledged to the performing of the yamas.[1] (1)

This great sage, who subdued all his senses, and who walked on the right road, came, on his wandering from village to village, to the town of Benares. (2)

There outside of Benares he took up his lodgings in a pleasant park; there he took up his abode in a pure place to live and sleep in. (3)

At the same time a Brāhmaṇa, versed in the Vēdas, Vijayaghōṣa by name, offered a sacrifice in that town. (4)

Now this houseless (monk) at the end of a fast of a month's duration, went to the sacrifice of Vijayaghōṣa to beg alms. (5)

The priest wanted to turn the approaching monk off: "I shall not give you alms, mendicant, beg somewhere else. (6)

"Priests who are versed in the Vēdas and are chaste as behoves offerers, who are versed in the Jyōtiṣāṅga[2] and are well grounded in the sacrificial science, who are able to save themselves. and others, such priests ought to be presented with food and all they desire." (7, 8)

When the great sage was thus refused by the priest, he was neither angry nor pleased, as he always strove for the highest good. (9)

Not to obtain food, or drink, or whatever else he wanted, but to save these people he spoke the following words: (10)

"You do not know what is most essential[3] in the Vēdas, nor in sacrifices, nor in the heavenly bodies,[4] nor in duties.[5] (11)

"Nor do you know those who are able to save themselves and others; but if you do, then speak out!" (12)

The priest did not make a reply to defend himself against his insinuation; but he and all there assembled joined their hands and questioned the great sage: (13)

"Tell us the most essential subject in the Vēdas, and tell us what is most essential in the sacrifice; tell us the first of the heavenly bodies, and tell us the best of dharmas. (14)

"Who are able to save themselves and others (*viz.* tell me). I ask you to solve this my doubt, O saint." (15)

"The most essential subject in the Vēdas is the agnihōtra, and that of the sacrifice is the purpose of the sacrifice;[6] the first of the heavenly bodies is the moon, and the best of dharmas is that of Kāśyapa (*i.e.* Riṣabha). (16)

"The beautiful (gods) with joined hands praise and worship the highest Lord (*i.e.* the Tīrthakara) as the planets, etc., (praise) the moon. (17)

"The ignorant (priests) pretend to know the sacrifice, those whose Brāhmanical excellence consists in (false) science; they shroud themselves in study and penance, being like fire covered by ashes. (18)

"He who is called by people a Brāhmaṇa and is worshipped like fire (is no true Brāhmaṇa). But him we call a true Brāhmaṇa, whom the wise point out as such. (19)

"He who has no worldly attachment after entering the order, who does not repent of having become a monk,[7] and who takes delight in the noble words, him we call a Brāhmaṇa. (20)

"He who is exempt from love, hatred, and fear, (and who shines forth) like burnished gold, purified in fire,[8] him we call a Brāhmaṇa. (21)

"A lean, self-subduing ascetic, who reduces his flesh and blood, who is pious and has reached Nirvāṇa, him we call a Brāhmaṇa. (22)

"He who thoroughly knows living beings, whether they move or not, and does not injure them in any of the three ways,[9] him we call a Brāhmaṇa. (23)

"He who does not speak untruth from anger or for fun, from greed or from fear, him we call a Brāhmaṇa. (24)

"He who does not take anything that is not given him, be it sentient or not sentient, small or large, him we call a Brāhmaṇa. (25)

"He who does not carnally love divine, human, or animal beings, in thoughts, words, or acts, him we call a Brāhmaṇa. (26)

"He who is not defiled by pleasures as a lotus growing in the water is not wetted by it, him we call a Brāhmaṇa. (27)

"He who is not greedy, who lives unknown, who has no house and no property, and who has no friendship with householders, him we call a Brāhmaṇa. (28)

"He who has given up his former connections (with his parents, etc.), with his kinsmen and relations, and who is not given to pleasure, him we call a Brāhmaṇa. (29)

"The binding of animals (to the sacrificial pole), all the Vēdas, and sacrifices, being causes of sin, cannot save the sinner; for his works (or Karman) are very powerful. (30)

"One does not become a Śramaṇa by the tonsure, nor a Brāhmaṇa by the sacred syllable Ōṃ, nor a Muni by living in the woods, nor a Tāpasa by wearing (clothes of) Kuśa-grass and bark. (31)

"One becomes a Śramaṇa by equanimity, a Brāhmaṇa by chastity, a Muni by knowledge, and a Tāpasa by penance. (32)

"By one's actions one becomes a Brāhmaṇa, or a Kṣatriya, or a Vaiśya, or a Śūdra. (33)

"The Enlightened One has declared these (good qualities) through which one becomes a (true) Snātaka;[10] him who is exempt from all Karman, we call a Brāhmaṇa. (34)

"The most excellent twice-born men[11] who possess these good qualities, are able to save themselves and others." (35)

When thus his doubt had been solved, Vijayaghōṣa, the Brāhmaṇa, assented[12] to the great sage Jayaghōṣa and to his (speech). (36)

Vijayaghōṣa, pleased, folded his hands and spoke as follows: "You have well declared to me what true Brāhmaṇahood consists in. (37)

"You are a sacrificer of sacrifices, you are the most learned of those who know the Vēdas, you know the Jyōtiṣāṅga, you know perfectly the Law. (38)

"You are able to save yourself and others; therefore do us the honour to accept our alms, O best of monks." (39)

"I do not want any alms; but, O Brāhmaṇa, enter the order at once, lest you should be drifted about on the dreadful ocean of the Saṃsāra, whose eddies are dangers. (40)

"There is glue (as it were) in pleasure: those who are not given to pleasure, are not soiled by it; those who love pleasures, must wander about in the Saṃsāra; those who do not, will be liberated. (41)

"If you take two clods of clay, one wet, the other dry, and fling them against the wall, the wet one will stick to it. (42)

"Thus foolish men, who love pleasure, will be fastened (to Karman), but the passionless will not, even as the dry clod of clay (does not stick to the wall)." (43)

When Vijayaghōṣa had learned the excellent Law from the houseless Jayaghōṣa, he entered the order. (44)

Jayaghōṣa and Vijayaghōṣa both annihilated their Karman by self-control and penance, and reached the highest perfection. (45)

Thus I say.

Twenty-Sixth Lecture: The Correct Behaviour

I shall declare the correct behaviour (sāmāchārī) which causes freedom from all misery; by practising it the Nirgranthas have crossed the ocean of Saṃsāra. (1)

The correct behaviour of monks consists of (the following) ten parts: 1. āvaśyikā; 2. naiṣēdhikī; 3. āpṛcchanā; 4. pratipṛcchanā; 5. chandanā; 6. icchākāra; 7. mithyākāra; 8. tathākāra; 9. abhyutthāna; 10. upasampad. (2-4)

The āvaśyikā is required when he leaves a room (or the presence of other monks on some necessary business); the naiṣēdhikī, on entering a place; āpṛcchanā, (or asking the superior's permission) for what he is to do himself; pratipṛcchanā, for what somebody else is to do; chandanā, (or placing at the disposal of other monks) the things one has got; icchākāra, in the execution (of one's intention by oneself or somebody else); mithyākāra, in the blaming oneself (for sins committed); tathākāra, (assent) in making a promise; abhyutthāna, in serving those who deserve respect; and upasampad, in placing oneself under another teacher. Thus the twice fivefold behaviour has been declared. (5-7)

After sunrise during the first quarter (of the first Pauruṣī)[1] he should inspect (and clean) his things and pay his respects to the superior. (8)

Then, with his hands joined, he should ask him:

"What shall I do now? I want to be employed, sir, in doing some work or in studying." (9)

If he is ordered to do some work, he should do it without tiring; if he is ordered to study, he should do it without allowing himself to be affected by any pains. (10)

A clever monk should divide the day into four (equal) parts (called pauruṣī), and fulfil his duties (uttaraguṇa) in all four parts. (11)

In the first Pauruṣī he should study, in the second he should meditate, in the third he should go on his begging-tour, and in the fourth he should study again. (12)

In the month āṣāḍha the Pauruṣī (of the night) contains two feet (pada);[2] in the month Pauṣa, four; in the months Chaitra and Aśvayuja, three. (13)

(The Pauruṣī) increases or decreases a digit[3] (aṅgula) every week, two digits every fortnight, four digits every month. (14)

The dark fortnight of āṣāḍha, Bhādrapada, Kārttika, Pauṣa, Phālguna, and Vaiśākha are known as avamarātrās.[4] (15)

In the quarter of the year comprising the three months Jyēṣṭhāmūla, āṣāḍha, and Śrāvaṇa, the (morning-) inspection is to last six digits (beyond ¼ Pauruṣī); in the second quarter, eight; in the third, ten; in the fourth, eight.[5] (16)

A clever monk should divide the night too into four parts, and fulfil his duties (uttaraguṇa) in all four parts. (17)

In the first Pauruṣī he should study, in the second he should meditate, in the third he should leave off sleep, and in the fourth he should study again. (18)

When the nakṣatra which leads the night[6] has reached the first quarter of the heaven, at dawn he should cease to study. (19)

When a small part of the quarter is left,[7] in which the (leading) nakṣatra stands, during that space of time, being considered intermediate[8] (between two) days, a monk should watch. (20)

In the first quarter (of the first Pauruṣī) he should inspect (and clean) his things, pay his respects to his superior, and then begin to study, not allowing himself to be affected by any pains.[9] (21)

In the (last) quarter of the first Pauruṣī, after paying his respect to the Guru, a monk should inspect his almsbowl, without, however, performing the Kāla-pratikramaṇa.[10] (22)

He should first inspect his mouth-cloth,[11] then his broom,[12] and taking the broom in his hand he should inspect his cloth. (23)

Standing upright he holds his cloth firmly and inspects it first leisurely, then he spreads it, and at last he wipes it. (24)

(He should spread the cloth) without shaking or crushing it, in such a way as to make the folds disappear, and to avoid friction of its parts against each other; he should fold it up six times in length, and nine times in breadth, and then he should remove living beings with his hand (spreading the cloth on the palm of his hand).[13] (25)

He must avoid want of attention: 1. in beginning his work; 2. in taking up the corners of the cloth; 3. in folding it up; 4. in shaking out the dust; 5. in putting it down (on some other piece of cloth); 6. in sitting upon the haunches.[14] (26)

(One must further avoid) to hold the cloth loosely, or at one corner, or so as to let it flap, or so as to subject it to friction, or so as to shake it in different ways, or if one has made a mistake in the number of foldings (see verse 25) to count (aloud or with the help of the fingers, etc.).[15] (27)

There should be neither too little nor too much of inspection, nor an exchange (of the things to be inspected); this is the right way to do (the inspection), all other methods are wrong:— (28)

(This is) if one engaged in inspecting his things converses or gossips (with anybody), renounces something,[16] teaches another his lesson, or receives his own lesson from another, (he neglects his inspection). (29)

He who is careful in the inspection, protects the six kinds of living beings, *viz.* the earth-bodies, water-bodies, fire-bodies, wind-bodies, plants, and animals. (30)

He who is careless in the inspection, injures the six kinds of living beings (just enumerated).[17] (31)

In the third Paurușī he should beg food and drink, (he may do so) for any of the following six reasons: (32)

1. To prevent an illness; 2. to serve the Guru; 3. to be able to comply with the rules about walking;[18] 4. to be able to comply with the rules of self-control;[19] 5. to save one's life; 6. to be able to meditate on the Law. (33)

A zealous Nirgrantha or Nirgranthī may omit to beg food for the following six reasons, when it will not be considered a transgression of his duties: (34)

1. In case of illness; 2. in case of a disaster; 3. to preserve one's chastity and the Guptis; 4. out of compassion for living beings; 5. in the interest of penance; 6. to make an end of one's life.[20] (35)

Taking his whole outfit a monk should inspect it with his eye; he then may walk about, but not beyond half a Yōjana. (36)

In the fourth Paurușī he should put away his almsbowl (after having eaten his meal), and then begins his study which reveals all existent things. (37)

In the last quarter of the fourth Paurușī he should pay his reverence to the Guru, and after having performed Kāla-pratikramaṇa,[21] he should inspect his lodging. (38)

A zealous monk should also inspect the place where to discharge his excrements and urine, and then (till the sun sets) he should go through Kāyōtsarga without allowing himself to be affected by any pains. (39)

Then he should, in due order, reflect on all transgressions he has committed during the day, with regard to knowledge, faith, and conduct. (40)

Having finished Kāyōtsarga, and paid his reverence to the Guru, he should, in due order, confess his transgressions committed during the day. (41)

Then having recited the Pratikramaṇa Sūtra,[22] and having annihilated his sins, he should pay his reverence to the Guru (asking absolution),[23] and go through Kāyōtsarga without allowing himself to be affected by any pains. (42)

Having finished Kāyōtsarga, and paid his reverence to the Guru, he should pronounce the customary (three) praises, and then wait for the proper time. (43)

In the first Paurușī (of the night) he should study; in the second he should meditate; in the third he should leave off sleep; and in the fourth he should study again.[24] (44)

In the fourth Paurușī he should wait for the proper time and then begin to study without waking the householders. (45)

In the last quarter of the fourth Paurușī he should pay his reverence to the Guru, and performing Kāla-pratikramaṇa[25] he should wait for the proper time. (46)

When the (time for) Kāyōtsarga has arrived, he should go through it, without allowing himself to be affected by any pains. (47)

Then he should, in due order, reflect on all transgressions he has committed during the night with regard to knowledge, faith, and conduct. (48)

Having finished Kāyōtsarga and paid his reverence to the Guru, he should, in due order, confess his transgressions committed during the night. (49)

Then having recited the Pratikramaṇa Sūtra etc. (see verse 41). (50)

He should consider what kind of austerities he will undertake. Having finished his Kāyōtsarga, he pays his reverence to the Guru. (51)

Having finished Kāyōtsarga and paid his reverence to the Guru, he should practise those austerities which he has decided upon, and praise the perfected saints. (52)

Thus has been summarily declared the correct behaviour, by practising which many souls have crossed the ocean of Saṃsāra. (53)

Thus I say.

Twenty-Seventh Lecture: The Bad Bullocks

There was a Sthavira and Gaṇadhara,[1] the learned sage Garga. This leader of the Gaṇa once made the following reflections: (1)

"He who rides in a car, crosses a wilderness; he who rides, as it were, in (the car of) religious exercise, crosses the Saṃsāra. (2)

"But he who puts bad bullocks[2] before his car, will be tired out with beating them; he will feel vexation, and his goad will be broken (at last). (3)

"(A bad bullock) will bite its mate in the tail; it will wound the other;[3] it will break the pin of the yoke,[4] or it will leave the road. (4)

"It will fall down on its side, or sit down, or lie down; it will jump up or caper, or it will obstinately make for a young cow. (5)

"It will furiously advance with its head lowered for an attack, or angrily go backward; it will stand still as if dead, or run at full speed. (6)

"The cursed beast[5] will rend asunder the rope, or in its unruliness break the yoke; and roaring it will break loose and run off. (7)

"Just as bad bullocks are when put before a car, so are bad pupils when yoked, as it were, to the car of the Law; they break down through want of zeal. (8)

"Some attach great importance[6] to their success; some to their good fare; some to their comfort; some nurse their anger. (9)

"Some are averse to begging; some are afraid of insults and are stuck up; (how can) I convince them by reasons and arguments[7] (?) (10)

"(A bad pupil) makes objections, and points out (imagined) difficulties; he frequently acts in opposition to the words of the superiors. (11)

"(He will say if sent to a lady): "She does not know me, she will give me nothing; I suppose she will be gone out; send some other monk there." (12)

"If sent on an errand, they do not do what they were bidden,[8] but stroll about wherever they like; or deporting themselves like servants of the king,[9] they knit their brows (when speaking to other people). (13)

"After they have been instructed, admitted into the order, and nourished with food and drink, they disperse in all directions like geese whose wings have grown." (14)

Now this driver (*viz.* Garga), who had to deal with bad bullocks, thought: "What have I to do with bad pupils? I am disheartened. (15)

"As are bad pupils, so are bad bullocks; I shall leave these lazy donkeys, and shall practise severe austerities." (16)

That noble man, who was full of kindness, grave, and always meditating, wandered about on the earth, leading a virtuous life. (17)

Thus I say.

Twenty-Eighth Lecture: The Road To Final Deliverance

Learn the true road leading to final deliverance, which the Jinas have taught; it depends on four causes and is characterised by right knowledge and faith. (1)

I. Right knowledge; II. Faith; III. Conduct; and IV. Austerities; this is the road taught by the Jinas who possess the best knowledge. (2)

Right knowledge, faith, conduct, and austerities; beings who follow this road, will obtain beatitude. (3)

I. Knowledge is fivefold: 1. Śruta, knowledge derived from the sacred books; 2. ābhinibōdhika, perception;[1] 3. Avadhi, supernatural knowledge; 4. Manaḥparyāya,[2] knowledge of the thoughts of other people; 5. Kēvala, the highest, unlimited knowledge. (4)

This is the fivefold knowledge. The wise ones have taught the knowledge of substances, qualities, and all developments.[3] (5)

Substance is the substrate of qualities; the qualities are inherent in one substance; but the characteristic of developments is that they inhere in either (*viz.* substances or qualities). (6)

Dharma, Adharma, space, time, matter, and souls (are the six kinds of substances[4]); they make up this world, as has been taught by the Jinas who possess the best knowledge. (7)

Dharma, Adharma, and space are each one substance only; but time, matter, and souls are an infinite number of substances. (8)

The characteristic of Dharma is motion, that of Adharma immobility, and that of space,[5] which contains all other substances, is to make room (for everything).[6] (9)

The characteristic of time is duration,[7] that of soul the realisation[8] of knowledge, faith, happiness, and misery. (10)

The characteristic of Soul is knowledge, faith, conduct, austerities, energy, and realisation (of its developments). (11)

The characteristic of matter is sound, darkness, lustre (of jewels, etc.), light, shade, sunshine; colour, taste, smell, and touch. (12)

The characteristic of development is singleness, separateness,[9] number, form, conjunction, and disjunction. (13)

1. jīva, Soul; 2. ajīva, the inanimate things; 3. bandha, the binding of the soul by Karman; 4. puṇya, merit; 5. pāpa, demerit; 6. āsrava, that which causes the soul to be affected by sins; 7. saṃvara, the prevention of āsrava by watchfulness; 8. the annihilation of Karman; 9. final deliverance: these are the nine truths (or categories). (14)

He who verily believes the true teaching of the (above nine) fundamental truths, possesses righteousness. (15)

II. Faith is produced by 1. nisarga, nature; 2. upadēśa, instruction; 3. ājñā, command; 4. sūtra, study of the sūtras; 5. bīja, suggestion; 6. abhigama, comprehension of the meaning of the sacred lore; 7. vistāra, complete course of study; 8. kriyā, religious exercise; 9. saṃkṣēpa, brief exposition; 10. dharma, the Law. (16)

1. He who truly comprehends, by a spontaneous effort of his mind,[10] (the nature of) soul, inanimate things, merit, and demerit, and who puts an end to sinful influences,[11] (believes by) nature. (17)

He who spontaneously believes the four truths (explicitly mentioned in the last verse), which the

2. But he who believes these truths, having learned them from somebody else, either a chadmastha[12] or a Jina, believes by instruction. (19)

3. He who has got rid of love, hate, delusion, and ignorance, and believes because he is told to do so, believes by command. (20)

4. He who obtains righteousness by (the study of) the Sūtras, either Angās or other works,[13] believes by the study of Sūtras. (21)

5. He who by correctly comprehending one truth arrives at the comprehension of more—just as a drop of oil expands on the surface of water—believes by suggestion. (22)

6. He who truly knows the sacred lore, *viz.* the eleven Angās, the Prakīrṇas,[14] and the Dṛṣṭivāda, believes by the comprehension of the sacred lore. (23)

7. He who understands the true nature of all substances by means of all proofs (pramāṇa) and nayas,[15] believes by a complete course of study. (24)

8. He who sincerely performs (all duties implied) by right knowledge, faith, and conduct, by asceticism and discipline, and by all Samitis and Guptis, believes by religious exercise. (25)

9. He who though not versed in the sacred doctrines[16] nor acquainted with other systems,[17] holds no wrong doctrines, believes by brief exposition. (26)

10. He who believes in the truth[18] of the realities,[19] the Sūtras, and conduct, as it has been explained by the Jinas, believes by the Law. (27)

Right belief depends on the acquaintance with truth,[20] on the devotion to those who know the truth, and on the avoiding of schismatical and heretical tenets. (28)

There is no (right) conduct without right belief,[21] and it must be cultivated (for obtaining) right faith; righteousness and conduct originate together, or righteousness precedes (conduct). (29)

Without (right) faith there is no (right) knowledge, without (right) knowledge there is no virtuous conduct,[22] without virtues there is no deliverance,[23] and without deliverance there is no perfection. (30)

(The excellence of faith depends on the following) eight points: 1. that one has no doubts (about the truth of the tenets); 2. that one has no preference (for heterodox tenets); 3. that one does not doubt its saving qualities;[24] 4. that one is not shaken in the right belief (because heretical sects are more prosperous); 5. that one praises (the pious); 6. that one encourages (weak brethren); 7. that one supports or loves the confessors of the Law; 8. that one endeavours to exalt it. (31)

III. Conduct, which produces the destruction of all Karman, is 1. sāmāyika,[25] the avoidance of everything sinful; 2. chēdōpasthāpana, the initiation of a novice; 3. parihāraviśuddhika, purity produced by peculiar austerities;[26] 4. sūkṣma samparāya, reduction of desire; 5. akaṣāya yathākhyāta, annihilation of sinfulness according to the precepts of the Arhats, as well in the case of a chadmastha as of a Jina. (32, 33)

IV. Austerities are twofold: external and internal; both external and internal austerities are sixfold. (34) By knowledge one knows things, by faith one believes in them, by conduct one gets (freedom from Karman), and by austerities one reaches purity. (35)

Having by control and austerities destroyed their Karman, great sages, whose purpose is to get rid of all misery, proceed to (perfection).

Thus I say.

Twenty-Ninth Lecture: The Exertion in Righteousness

O long-lived (Jambūsvāmin)! I (Sudharman) have heard the following discourse from the venerable (Mahāvīra).

Here, forsooth, the Venerable Ascetic Mahāvīra, of the Kaśyapa Gōtra, has delivered this lecture called the exertion in righteousness. Many creatures, who truly believe in the subject (taught in this lecture), put their faith in it, give credence to it, accept it, practise it, comply with it, study it, understand it, learn it, and act up to it according to the precept (of the Jinas)[1]—have obtained perfection, enlightenment, deliverance, final beatitude, and have put an end to all misery.

This lecture treats of the following subjects:

1. saṃvēga, longing for liberation;

2. nirvēda, disregard of worldly objects;

3. dharmaśraddhā, desire of the Law;

4. gurusādharmikaśuśrūṣaṇā, obedience to co-religionists and to the Guru.

5. ālōchanā, confession of sins before the Guru;

6. nindā, repenting of one's sins to oneself;

7. garhā, repenting of one's sins before the Guru;

8. sāmāyika, moral and intellectual purity of the soul;

9. chaturviṃśatistava, adoration of the twenty-four Jinas;

10. vandana, paying reverence to the Guru;

11. pratikramaṇa, expiation of sins;

12. kāyōtsarga, a particular position of the body;
13. pratyākhyāna, self-denial;
14. stavastutimaṅgala, praises and hymns;
15. kālasya pratyupēkṣaṇā, keeping the right time;
16. prāyaśchittakaraṇa, practising penance;
17. kṣamāpana, begging forgiveness;
18. svādhyāya, study;
19. vāchanā, recital of the sacred texts;
20. paripṛcchanā, questioning (the teacher);
21. parāvartanā, repetition;
22. anuprēkṣā, pondering;
23. dharmakathā, religious discourse;
24. śrutasyārādhanā, acquisition of sacred knowledge;
25. ēkāgramanaḥsannivēśanā, concentration of thoughts;
26. saṃyama, control;
27. tapas, austerities;
28. vyavadāna, cutting off the Karman;
29. sukhāśāta, renouncing pleasure;
30. apratibaddhatā, mental independence;
31. vichitraśayanāsanasēvanā, using unfrequented lodgings and beds;
32. vinivartanā, turning from the world;
33. sambhōgapratyākhyāna, renouncing collection of alms in one district only;
34. upadhipratyākhyāna, renouncing articles of use;
35. āhārapratyākhyāna, renouncing food;
36. kaṣāyapratyākhyāna, conquering the passions;
37. yōgapratyākhyāna, renouncing activity;
38. śarīrapratyākhyāna, renouncing the body;
39. sahāyapratyākhyāna, renouncing company;
40. bhaktapratyākhyāna, renouncing all food;
41. sadbhāvapratyākhyāna, perfect renunciation;
42. pratirūpatā, conforming to the standard;
43. vaiyāvṛtya, doing service;

44. sarvaguṇasampūrṇatā, fulfilling all virtues;
45. vītarāgatā, freedom from passion;
46. kṣānti, patience;
47. mukti, freedom from greed;
48, ārjava, simplicity;
49. mārdava, humility;
50. bhāvasatya, sincerity of mind;
51. karaṇasatya, sincerity of religious practice;
52. yōgasatya, sincerity of acting;
53. manōguptatā, watchfulness of the mind;
54. vāg-guptatā, watchfulness of the speech;
55. kāyaguptatā, watchfulness of the body;
56. manaḥsamādhāraṇā, discipline of the mind;
57. vāksamādhāraṇā, discipline of the speech;
58. kāyasamādhāraṇā, discipline of the body;
59. jñānasampannatā, possession of knowledge;
60. darśanasampannatā, possession of faith;
61. chāritrasampannatā, possession of conduct;
62. śrōtrēndriyanigraha, subduing the ear;
63. chakṣurindriyanigraha, subduing the eye;
64. ghrāṇēndriyanigraha, subduing the organ of smell;
65. jihvēndriyanigraha, subduing the tongue;
66. sparśanēndriyanigraha, subduing the organ of touch;
67. krōdhavijaya, conquering anger;
68. mānavijaya, conquering pride;
69. māyāvijaya, conquering deceit;
70. lōbhavijaya, conquering greed;
71. prēmadvēṣamithyādarśaṇavijaya, conquering love, hate, and wrong belief;
72. śailēśī, stability;
73. akarmatā, freedom from Karman.

1. Sir, what does the soul obtain by the longing for liberation? By the longing for liberation the soul obtains an intense desire of the Law; by an intense desire of the Law he quickly arrives at an (increased) longing

for liberation; he destroys anger, pride, deceit, and greed, which reproduce themselves infinitely; he acquires no (bad) Karman, and ridding himself of wrong belief which is the consequence of the latter, he becomes possessed of right faith; by the purity of faith some will reach perfection after one birth; nobody, however, who has got this purity, will be born more than thrice before he reaches perfection. (1)

2. Sir, what does the soul obtain by disregard of worldly objects?[2] By disregard of worldly objects the soul quickly feels disgust for pleasures enjoyed by gods, men, and animals; he becomes indifferent to all objects; thereby he ceases to engage in any undertakings, in consequence of which he leaves the road of Saṃsāra and enters the road to perfection. (2)

3. Sir,[3] what does the soul obtain by the desire of the Law? By the desire of the Law the soul becomes indifferent to pleasures and happiness to which he was attached; he abandons the life of householders, and as a houseless monk he puts an end to all pains of body and mind, which consist in (the suffering of) cutting, piercing, union (with unpleasant things), etc.; and he obtains unchecked happiness. (3)

4. By obedience to co-religionists and to the Guru the soul obtains discipline (vinaya). By discipline and avoidance of misconduct (towards the teacher[4]) he avoids being reborn as a denizen of hell, an animal, a (low) man, or a (bad) god; by zealous praise of, devotion to, and respect for (the Guru) he obtains birth as a (good) man or god, gains perfection and beatitude, does all praiseworthy actions prescribed by discipline, and prevails upon others to adopt discipline. (4)

5. By confession of sins (before the Guru) the soul gets rid of the thorns, as it were, of deceit, misapplied austerities,[5] and wrong belief, which obstruct the way to final liberation and cause an endless migration of the soul; he obtains simplicity, whereby the soul which is free from deceit does not acquire that Karman which results in his having a carnal desire for a woman or eunuch,[6] and annihilates such Karman as he had acquired before. (5)

6. By repenting of one's sins to oneself the soul obtains repentance, and becoming indifferent by repentance he prepares for himself an (ascending) scale of virtues,[7] by which he destroys the Karman resulting

from delusion. (6)

7. By repenting of one's sins before the Guru the soul obtains humiliation; feeling humiliated, he will leave off all blameable occupations,[8] and apply himself to praiseworthy occupations, whereby a houseless monk will stop infinite disabling[9] developments. (7)

8. By moral and intellectual purity (literally, equilibrium) the soul ceases from sinful occupations. (8)

9. By the adoration of the twenty-four Jinas the soul arrives at purity of faith. (9)

10. By paying reverence (to the Guru) the soul destroys such Karman as leads to birth in low families, and acquires such Karman as leads to birth in noble families; he wins the affection of people, which results in his being looked upon as an authority, and he brings about general goodwill. (10)

11. By expiation of sins he obviates transgressions of the vows; thereby he stops the āsravas, preserves a pure conduct, practises the eight articles,[10] does not neglect (the practice of control), and pays great attention to it. (11)

12. By Kāyōtsarga he gets rid of past and present (transgressions which require) Prāyaśchitta;[11] thereby his mind is set at ease like a porter who is eased of his burden; and engaging in praiseworthy contemplation he enjoys happiness. (12)

13. By self-denial he shuts, as it were, the doors of the āsravas; by self-denial he prevents desires rising in him; by prevention of desires he becomes, as it were, indifferent and cool towards all objects. (13)

14. By praises and hymns he obtains the wisdom consisting in knowledge, faith, and conduct; thereby he gains such improvement, that he will put an end to his worldly existence,[12] (or) be born afterwards in one of the Kalpas and Vimānas.[13] (14)

15. By keeping the right time he destroys the Karman which obstructs right knowledge. (15)

16. By practising Prāyaśchitta he gets rid of sins, and commits no transgressions; he who correctly practises Prāyaśchitta, gains the road and the reward of the road,[14] he wins the reward of good conduct. (16)

17. By begging forgiveness he obtains happiness of mind; thereby he acquires a kind disposition towards all kinds of living beings;[15] by this

kind disposition he obtains purity of character and freedom from fear. (17)

18. By study he destroys the Karman which obstructs right knowledge. (18)

19. By the recital of the sacred texts he obtains destruction of Karman, and contributes to preserve the sacred lore, whereby he acquires the Law of the Tīrtha,[16] which again leads him to the complete destruction of Karman, and to the final annihilation of worldly existence. (19)

20. By questioning (the teacher) he arrives at a correct comprehension of the Sūtra and its meaning, and he puts an end to the Karman which produces doubts and delusion. (20)

21. By repetition he reproduces the sounds (*i.e.* syllables) and commits them to memory. (21)

22. By pondering (on what he has learned) he loosens the firm hold which the seven kinds of Karman, except the āyuṣka[17] (have upon the soul); he shortens their duration when it was to be a long one; he mitigates their power when it was intense; (he reduces their sphere of action when it was a wide one);[18] he may either acquire āyuṣka-karman or not, but he no more accumulates Karman which produces unpleasant feelings, and he quickly crosses the very large forest of the fourfold Saṃsāra, which is without beginning and end. (22)

23. By religious discourses he obtains destruction of the Karman; by religious discourses he exalts the creed, and by exalting the creed he acquires Karman, which secures, for the future, permanent bliss. (23)

24. By acquisition of sacred knowledge he destroys ignorance, and will not be corrupted by worldliness. (24)

25. By concentration of his thoughts he obtains stability of the mind. (25)

26. By control he obtains freedom from sins. (26)

27. By austerities he cuts off the Karman.[19] (27)

28. By cutting off the Karman he obtains (the fourth stage of pure meditation characterised by) freedom from actions, by doing no actions he will obtain perfection, enlightenment, deliverance, and final beatitude, and will put an end to all misery. (28)

29. By renouncing pleasures he obtains freedom from false longing,

whereby he becomes compassionate, humble, free from sorrow, and destroys the Karman produced by delusion regarding conduct. (29)

30. By mental independence he gets rid of attachment, whereby he will concentrate his thoughts (on the Law), and will for ever be without attachment and fondness (for worldly things). (30)

31. By using unfrequented lodgings and beds he obtains the Gupti of conduct, whereby he will use allowed food, be steady in his conduct, be exclusively delighted with (control), obtain a yearning for deliverance, and cut off the tie of the eightfold Karman. (31)

32. By turning from the world he will strive to do no bad actions, and will eliminate his already acquired Karman by its destruction; then he will cross the forest of the fourfold Saṃsāra. (32)

33. By renouncing collection of alms in one district only[20] he overcomes obstacles;[21] unchecked by them he exerts himself to attain liberation; he is content with the alms he gets, and does not hope for, care for, wish, desire, or covet those of a fellow-monk; not envying other monks he takes up a separate, agreeable lodging.[22] (33)

34. By renouncing articles of use[23] he obtains successful study; without articles of use he becomes exempt from desires, and does not suffer misery. (34)

35. By renouncing (forbidden) food he ceases to act for the sustenance of his life; ceasing to act for the sustenance of his life he does not suffer misery when without food. (35)

36. By conquering his passions he becomes free from passions; thereby he becomes indifferent to happiness and pains. (36)

37. By renouncing activity he obtains inactivity, by ceasing to act he acquires no new Karman, and destroys the Karman he had acquired before. (37)

38. By renouncing his body he acquires the pre-eminent virtues of the Siddhas, by the possession of which he goes to the highest region of the universe, and becomes absolutely happy. (38)

39. By renouncing company he obtains singleness; being single and concentrating his mind, he avoids disputes, quarrels, passions, and censoriousness, and he acquires a high degree of control, of Saṃvara, and of carefulness.[24] (39)

40. By renouncing all food he prevents his being born again many

hundreds of times. (40)

41. By perfect renunciation[25] he enters the final (fourth stage of pure meditation), whence there is no return; a monk who is in that state, destroys the four remnants of Karman which even a Kēvalin possesses, *viz.* vēdanīya, āyuṣka, nāman, and gōtra;[26] and then he will put an end to all misery. (41)

42. By conforming to the standard of monks[27] he obtains ease, thereby he will be careful, wear openly the excellent badges of the order, be of perfect righteousness, possess firmness and the Samitis, inspire all beings with confidence, mind but few things,[28] subdue his senses, and practise, in a high degree, the Samitis and austerities. (42)

43. By doing service he acquires the Karman which brings about for him the nāman and gōtra of a Tīrthakara. (43)

By fulfilling all virtues he secures that he will not be born again; thereby he will become exempt from pains of the body and mind. (44)

45. By freedom from passion he cuts off the ties of attachment and desire; thereby he becomes indifferent to all agreeable and disagreeable sounds, touches, colours, and smells. (45)

46. By patience he overcomes troubles. (46)

47. By freedom from greed he obtains voluntary poverty, whereby he will become inaccessible to desire for property. (47)

48. By simplicity he will become upright in actions, thoughts, and speech, and he will become veracious; thereby he will truly practise the Law. (48)

49. By humility he will acquire freedom from self-conceit; thereby he will become of a kind and meek disposition, and avoid the eight kinds of pride. (49)

50. By sincerity of mind he obtains purity of mind, which will cause him to exert himself for the fulfilment of the Law which the Jinas have proclaimed; and he will practise the Law in the next world too. (50)

51. By sincerity in religious practice he obtains proficiency in it; being proficient in it he will act up to his words. (51)

52. By sincerity of acting he will become pure in his actions. (52)

53. By watchfulness[29] of the mind he concentrates his thoughts; thereby he truly practises control. (53)

54. By watchfulness of speech he keeps free from prevarication; thereby he enables his mind to act properly. (54)

55. By watchfulness of the body he obtains Saṃvara;[30] thereby he prevents sinful āsravas. (55)

56. By discipline of the mind he obtains concentration of his thoughts; thereby he obtains development of knowledge, which produces righteousness and annihilates wrong belief. (56)

57. By discipline of the speech he obtains development of faith, whereby he acquires facility of becoming enlightened, and destroys preventing causes. (57)

58. By discipline of the body he obtains development of conduct, which causes him to conduct himself according to the regulation; thereby he destroys the four remnants of Karman which even a Kēvalin possesses;[31] after that he obtains perfection, enlightenment, deliverance, and final beatitude, and he puts an end to all misery. (58)

59. By possession of knowledge he acquires an understanding of words and their meaning; thereby he will not perish in the forest of the fourfold Saṃsāra; as a needle with its thread will not be lost, thus the soul possessing the sacred lore[32] will not be lost in the Saṃsāra; he performs all prescribed actions relating to knowledge, discipline, austerities, and conduct, and well versed in his own and in heterodox creeds he will become invincible. (59)

60. By possession of faith he annihilates wrong belief which is the cause of worldly existence, and he will not lose his inner light; but he endues his Self with the highest knowledge and faith, and purifies it.[33] (60)

61. By possession of conduct he obtains a stability like that of the king of mountains[34] (*viz.* Mēru), whereby a houseless monk destroys the four remnants of Karman which even a Kēvalin possesses; after that he obtains perfection, enlightenment, deliverance, and final beatitude, and puts an end to all misery. (61)

62. By subduing the organ of hearing he overcomes his delight with or aversion to all pleasant or unpleasant sounds, he acquires no Karman produced thereby, and destroys the Karman he had acquired before. (62)

63-66. (All this applies also to his) subduing the organs of sight, of smelling, of tasting, and of touch (with regard to) pleasant colours, smells, tastes, and touches. (63-66)

67. By conquering anger he obtains patience; he acquires no Karman productive of anger,[35] and destroys the Karman he had acquired before. (67)

68. By conquering pride he obtains simplicity, etc. (as in 67, substituting pride for anger). (68)

69. By conquering deceit he obtains humility, etc. (as in 67, substituting deceit for anger). (69)

70. By conquering greed he obtains content, etc. (as in 67, substituting greed for anger). (70)

71. By conquering love, hate, and wrong belief he exerts himself for right knowledge, faith, and conduct, then he will cut off the fetters of the eightfold Karman; he will first destroy the twenty-eight kinds[36] of Karman, which are productive of delusion; (then) the five kinds of obstruction to right knowledge,[37] the nine kinds of obstruction to right faith,[38] and the five kinds of obstacles (called Antarāya): the last three remnants of Karman he destroys simultaneously; afterwards he obtains absolute knowledge and faith, which is supreme, full, complete, unchecked, clear, faultless, and giving light (or penetrating) the whole universe; and while he still acts,[39] he acquires but such Karman as is inseparable from religious acts;[40] the pleasant feelings (produced by it) last but two moments: in the first moment it is acquired, in the second it is experienced, and in the third it is destroyed; this Karman is produced, comes into contact (with the soul), takes rise, is experienced, and is destroyed; for all time to come he is exempt from Karman. (71)

72. Then[41] when his life is spent up to less than half a muhūrta, he discontinues to act, and enters upon the (third degree of) pure meditation,[42] from which there is no relapse (to lower degrees), and which requires most subtile functions only (of his organs); he first stops the functions of his mind, then the functions of speech, then those of the body, at last he ceases to breathe. During the time required for pronouncing five short syllables, he is engaged in the final pure meditation, in which all functions (of his organs) have ceased, and he simultaneously annihilates the four remnants of Karman, *viz.* vēdanīya, āyuṣka, nāman, and gōtra.[43] (72)

73. Then having, by all methods, got rid of his audārika, kārmaṇa (and taijasa) bodies, the soul takes the form of a straight line, goes in one moment, without touching anything and taking up no space, (upwards to the highest Akāśa), and there develops into its natural form, obtains perfection, enlightenment, deliverance, and final beatitude, and puts an end to all misery. (73)

This indeed is the subject of the lecture called exertion in righteousness, which the Venerable Ascetic Mahāvīra has told, declared, explained, demonstrated. (74)

Thus I say.

Thirtieth Lecture: The Road of Penance

Now hear with concentrated mind, how a monk destroys by austerities the bad Karman which he had acquired by love and hatred. (1)

By abstaining 1. from destroying life; 2. from lying; 3. from taking anything which is not given; 4. from all sexual indulgence; 5. from having any property; and 6. from eating at night, the soul becomes free from āsravas.[1] (2)

By possessing the five Samitis and the three Guptis, by freedom from passions, by subduing the senses, by vanquishing conceit,[2] and by avoiding delusions, the soul becomes free from āsravas. (3)

Hear attentively how a monk destroys (the Karman) acquired by love and hatred in the absence of the above-mentioned (virtues). (4)

As a large tank, when its supply of water has been stopped, gradually dries up by the consumption of the water and by evaporation, so the Karman of a monk, which he acquired in millions[3] of births, is annihilated by austerities, if there is no influx of bad Karman. (5, 6)

Austerities are of two kinds: external and internal; external austerities are of six kinds, and internal are of six kinds.[4] (7)

External austerities are:

1. anaśana, fasting; 2. avamōdarikā, abstinence;[5] 3. bhikṣācharyā, collecting alms; 4. rasaparityāga, abstention from dainty food; 5. kāyaklēśa, mortification of the flesh; 6. saṃlīnatā, taking care of one's limbs.[6] (8)

1. Fasting is of two kinds: *a*. itvara, temporary, and *b*. maraṇakāla,

fasting which precedes, and ends with death. Temporary fasting is either such in which a desire (for food) is present, or such in which no such desire exists. (9)

a. The temporary fasting is briefly of six kinds: 1. in the form of a line;[7] 2. in the form of a square; 3. in the form of a cube; 4. of a sixth power; 5. of a twelfth power; 6. of any arrangement. Temporary fasting (can be practised) for different objects which one has in mind. (10, 11)

b. Fasting which is to precede death, is of two kinds with regard to the motions of the body: with change (of position) and without change. (12)

And again it is twofold: admitting of relief,[8] or not; one may either leave the place (which one has chosen to die in), or not leave it; in both cases one may not take any food. (13)

2. Abstinence is briefly of five kinds: with regard to *a*. substance; *b*. place; *c*. time; *d*. state of mind; *e*. development. (14)

a. He who takes less food than he usually does,[9] in the extreme case but one mouthful, performs abstinence with regard to substance. (15)

b. (Place means) a village, a scotfree town,[10] a capital, a camp of merchants,[11] a mine, a settlement of a wild tribe,[12] a place with an earth wall,[13] a poor town,[14] a town with a harbour,[15] a large town,[16] an isolated town,[17] and an open town.[18] (16)

In a hermitage, a vihāra,[19] a halting-place for procession,[20] a resting-place for travellers,[21] a station of herdsmen, a camp on high ground, a caravan's camp, a fortified place of refuge. (17)

In gardens, on roads, in houses—all this is meant by place. In these and similar places he may (wander about). In this way he performs abstinence with regard to place. (18)

1. pēṭā, 2. ardhapēṭā, 3. gōmūtrikā, 4. pataṅgavīthikā, 5. śambūkāvartta, 6. āyataṃ-gatvā-pratyāgata.[22] (19)

c. Abstinence with reference to time (is observed by him) who goes about in that time of the four Paurușīs of the day (which he selects for that purpose). (20)

Or if he collects alms in a part of the third Paurușī, or in its last quarter, then he observes abstinence with reference to time. (21)

d. Abstinence with reference to state of mind (is observed by him) who accepts alms from a woman or man, from an adorned or unadorned person, from one of any age or dress, of any temper or colour: if that person does not change his disposition or condition.[23] (22, 23)

e. A monk who observes abstinence according to the particulars which have been enumerated with regard to substance, place, time, and state of mind, observes abstinence with regard to development[24] too. (24)

3. With regard to collecting alms there are the eight principal ways[25] how to collect them; the seven ēṣaṇās (or modes of begging) and other self-imposed restrictions. (25)

4. Abstention from dainty food means abstention from such highly nourishing[26] food and drink as milk, curds, ghee, etc. (26)

5. Mortification of the flesh consists in the different postures as Virāsana, etc., which benefit the soul, and which are difficult to perform. (27)

6. Using unfrequented lodgings and beds consists in living and sleeping in separate and unfrequented places where there are neither women nor cattle. (28)

Thus external austerities have been briefly explained; I shall now explain internal austerities in due order. (29)

Internal austerities are:

1. prāyaśchitta, expiation of sins;

2. viṇaya, politeness;

3. vaiyāvṛtya, serving the Guru;

4. svādhyāya, study;

5. dhyāna, meditation;

6. vyutsarga,[27] abandoning of the body. (30)

1. Expiation of sins is tenfold, what must be confessed,[28] etc.; this is to be strictly observed by a monk; this is called expiation of sins. (31)

2. Politeness consists in rising (from one's seat), folding of the hands, offering of a seat, loving the Guru, and cordial obedience. (32)

3. There are ten[29] kinds of service, as serving the āchārya, etc.;[30] doing service consists in giving one's assistance as well as one is able. (33)

4. Study is fivefold: 1. saying or learning one's lesson; 2. (questioning the teacher about it); 3. repetition; 4. pondering; 5. religious discourse. (34)

5. Abstaining to meditate on painful and sinful things,[31] one should, with a collected mind, engage in pure meditations on the Law; this the wise call meditation. (35)

6. If a monk remains motionless when lying down, sitting, or standing upright, this is called abandoning of the body, which is the sixth kind (of internal austerities). (36)

If a sage truly performs these two kinds of austerities, he will soon be thoroughly released from the Circle of Births. (37)

Thus I say.

Thirty-First Lecture: Mode of Life [1]

I shall declare the mode of life that benefits the soul; by practising it many souls have crossed the ocean of Saṃsāra. (1)

One should desist from one thing, and practise another: desist from neglect of self-control, and practise self-control. (2)

Love and hatred are two evils which produce bad Karman; if a monk always avoids them, he will not stand within the circle (of transmigration). (3)

A monk who always avoids the thrice threefold hurtful, conceited, and delusive acts,[2] will not stand in the circle (of transmigration). (4)

A monk who well bears calamities produced by gods, animals, or men, will not stand, etc. (5)

A monk who always avoids the (four) different kinds of praises,[3] passions, expressions (of the emotions),[4] and (of the four) meditations the two sinful ones, will not stand, etc. (6)

A monk who always exerts himself[5] with regard to the (five) vows, the (five) objects of sense, the (five) Samitis, and (five) actions,[6] will not stand, etc. (7)

A monk who always exerts himself with regard to the six lēśyās,[7] the six kinds of bodies, and the six (regular functions as) eating,[8] will not stand, etc. (8)

A monk who always exerts himself with regard to the (seven) rules of accepting alms,[9] and the seven causes of danger (to other men) will not stand, etc. (9)

A monk who always exerts himself with regard to the (eight) objects of pride,[10] to that which protects his chastity[11], and to the tenfold Law of the monks.[12] (10)

A monk who always exerts himself with regard to the (eleven) duties of the upāsakas, and the (twelve) duties of the bhikṣus,[13] will not stand, etc. (11)

A monk who always exerts himself with regard to the (thirteen) actions (productive of Karman), to the various (fourteen) kinds of living beings, and the (fifteen) places of punishment of the wicked,[14] will not stand, etc. (12)

A monk who always exerts himself with regard to the sixteen Gāthās,[15] and to the (seventeen kinds of) neglect of self-control, will not stand, etc. (13)

A monk who always exerts himself with regard to the (eighteen kinds of) continence, to the (nineteen) jñātādhyayanas,[16] and the (twenty) cases for not concentrating one's thoughts, will not, etc. (14)

A monk who always exerts himself with regard to the twenty-one forbidden[17] actions, and the twenty-two troubles,[18] will not stand, etc. (15)

A monk who always exerts himself with regard to the twenty-three (lectures of the) Sūtrakṛtāṅga, and to the gods whose number exceeds by an unit[19] (the number of the lectures of the Sūtrakṛtāṅga), will not stand, etc. (16)

A monk who always exerts himself with regard to the twenty-five clauses,[20] and (to the recitation of the twenty-six) chapters of the Daśās, etc.,[21] will not stand, etc. (17)

A monk who always exerts himself with regard to the (twenty-seven) virtues of the laity, and the (twenty-eight lectures of the) Prakalpa,[22] will not stand, etc. 08)

A monk who always exerts himself with regard to the (twenty-nine) causes of wrong knowledge, and the (thirty) causes of delusion, will not stand, etc. (19)

A monk who always exerts himself with regard to the (thirty-one) qualities of Siddhas, etc., the (thirty-two) Yogas,[23] and thirty-three āśātanās,[24] will not stand, etc. (20)

A clever monk who always exerts himself with regard to the above-mentioned points, will soon be thoroughly released from the Circle of Births (21)

Thus I say.

Thirty-Second Lecture: The Causes of Carelessness

With attentive mind hear me explain for your benefit the deliverance from the beginningless time, together with its causes,[1] and from all misery: a truly wholesome subject. (1)

By the teaching of true[2] knowledge, by the avoidance of ignorance and delusion, and by the destruction of love and hatred, one arrives at final deliverance which is nothing but bliss. (2)

This is the road to it: to serve the Gurus and the old (teachers), to avoid throughout fooliṣ people, to apply oneself earnestly to study, and to ponder zealously on the meaning of the Sūtras. (3)

A Śramaṇa engaged in austerities, who longs for righteousness,[3] should eat the proper quantity of allowed food, should select a companion of right understanding, and should live in a place suited to seclusion. (4)

If he does not meet with a clever companion who surpasses or equals him in virtue, he should live by himself, abstaining from sins and not devoted to pleasures. (5)

As the crane[4] is produced from an egg, and the egg is produced from a crane, so they call desire[5] the origin of delusion, and delusion the origin of desire. (6)

Love and hatred are caused by Karman, and they say that Karman has its origin in delusion; Karman is the root of birth and death, and birth and death they call misery. (7)

Misery ceases on the absence of delusion, delusion ceases on the absence of desire, desire ceases on the absence of greed, greed ceases on the absence of property. (8)

I shall explain in due order the means which must be adopted by him who wants to thoroughly uproot love, hatred, and delusion. (9)

Pleasant food[6] should not be enjoyed with preference, for it generally makes men over-strong;[7] and desires rush upon the strong, like birds upon a tree with sweet fruits. (10)

As in a forest, full of fuel, a fire fanned by the wind cannot be extinguished, so the fire (as it were) of the senses of him who eats as he lists; it does not benefit any chaste man. (11)

The mind of those who always live in unfrequented lodgings, who eat low food, and who subdue their senses, will not be attacked by the foe, Love, who is vanquished as disease is by medicine. (12)

As it is not safe for mice to live near the dwelling of a cat, so a chaste (monk) cannot stay in a house inhabited by women. (13)

A Śramaṇa, engaged in penance, should not allow himself to watch the shape, beauty, coquetry, laughter, prattle, gestures, and glances of women, nor retain a recollection of them in his mind. (14)

Not to look at, nor to long for, not to think of, nor to praise, womankind: this is becoming the meditation of the noble ones, and it is always wholesome to those who delight in chastity. (15)

Though those who possess the three Guptis, cannot be disturbed even by well-adorned goddesses, still it is recommended to monks to live by themselves, as this is wholesome in every way. (16)

To a man who longs for liberation, who is afraid of the Saṃsāra, and lives according to the Law, nothing in the world offers so many difficulties[8] as women who delight the mind of the ignorant. (17)

To those who have overcome the attachment (to women), all others will offer no difficulties;[9] even as to those who have crossed the great ocean, no river, though big like the Ganges, (will offer any difficulty). (18)

From desire of pleasure arises the misery of the whole world, the gods included; whatever misery of body and mind there is, the dispassionate will put an end to it. (19)

As the fruit of the Kimpāka[10] is beautiful in taste and colour, when eaten; but destroys the life when digested, (being) poison; similar in their effect are pleasures. (20)

A Śramaṇa, engaged in austerities, who longs for righteousness,[11] should not fix his thoughts on the pleasant objects of the senses, nor turn his mind from them, if they be unpleasant. (21)

"Colour" attracts the eye; it is the pleasant cause of Love, but the unpleasant cause of Hatred;[12] he who is indifferent to them (*viz.* colours), is called dispassionate. (22)

The eye perceives "colour," and "colour" attracts the eye; the cause of Love is pleasant, and the cause of Hatred is unpleasant. (23)

He who is passionately fond of "colours," will come to untimely ruin; just as an impassioned moth which is attracted by the light rushes into death. (24)

He who passionately hates (a colour), will at the same moment suffer pain. It is the fault of an undisciplined man that he is annoyed (by a colour); it is not the "colour" itself that annoys him. (25)

He who is very fond of a lovely "colour," hates all others; hence a fool will suffer misery, but a dispassionate sage is not affected by it. (26)

He who has a passion for "colours,"[13] will kill many movable and immovable beings; a passionate fool, intent on his personal interest, pains and torments those beings in many ways. (27)

How can a man who passionately desires "colours,"[14] be happy while he gets, keeps, uses, loses, and misses (those things). Even when he enjoys them, he is never satisfied. (28)

When he is not satisfied with those "colours," and his craving for them grows stronger and stronger, he will become discontented, and unhappy by dint of his discontent; misled by greed he will take another's property. (29)

When he is overcome by violent desire, takes another's property, and is not satisfied with those "colours" and their possession, then his deceit and falsehood increase on account of his greed; yet he will not get rid of his misery. (30)

After and before he has lied,[15] and when he is on the point of lying, he feels infinitely unhappy. Thus when he takes another's property, and is (after all) not satisfied by the "colours" (he has obtained), he becomes unhappy, and nobody will protect him.[16] (31)

How, then, can a man who is devoted to "colours," ever derive any happiness from anything? He suffers pain at the time of their enjoyment to procure which he had suffered misery. (32)

In the same way he who hates "colours," incurs a long succession of pains; when his mind is filled with hatred, he accumulates Karman which in the end again produces misery. (33)

But a man who is indifferent to "colours," is free from sorrows; though still in the Saṃsāra, he is not affected by that long succession of pains, just as the leaf of the Lotus (is not moistened) by water. (34)

"Sound" attracts the ear; it is the pleasant cause of Love, but the unpleasant cause of Hatred; he who is indifferent to them (*viz.* sounds), is called dispassionate. (35)

The ear perceives "sound," and "sound" attracts the ear; the cause of Love is pleasant, and the cause of Hatred is unpleasant. (36)

He who is passionately fond of "sounds," will come to untimely ruin; just as an impassioned deer allured (by a song) rushes into death, without being satisfied with the sound. (37)

He who passionately hates (a sound), will at the same moment suffer pain. It is the fault of an undisciplined man that he is annoyed (by a sound); it is not the "sound" itself that annoys him. (38)

He who is very fond of a lovely "sound," hates all others; hence a fool will suffer misery, but a dispassionate sage is not affected by it. (39)

He who has a passion for "sounds," will kill many movable and immovable beings; a passionate fool, intent on his personal interest, pains and torments those beings in many ways. (40)

How can a man who passionately desires "sounds," be happy while he gets, keeps, uses, loses, and misses (those things). Even when he enjoys them, he is never satisfied. (41)

When he is not satisfied with those "sounds," and his craving for them grows stronger and stronger, he will become discontented, and unhappy by dint of his discontent; misled by greed he will take another's property. (42)

When he is overcome by violent desire, takes another's property, and is not satisfied with those "sounds" and their possession, then his deceit and falsehood increase on account of his greed; yet he will not get rid of his misery. (43)

After and before he has lied, and when he is on the point of lying, he feels infinitely unhappy. Thus when he takes another's property, and is (after all) not satisfied by the "sounds" (he has obtained), he becomes unhappy, and nobody will protect him. (44)

How, then, can a man who is devoted to "sounds," ever derive any happiness from anything? He suffers pain at the time of their enjoyment to procure which he had suffered misery. (45)

In the same way he who hates "sounds," incurs a long succession of pains; when his mind is filled with hatred, he accumulates Karman which in the end again produces misery. (46)

But a man who is indifferent to "sounds," is free from sorrows;

though still in the Saṃsāra, he is not affected by that long succession of pains, just as the leaf of the Lotus (is not moistened) by water. (47)

"Smell" attracts the nose; it is the pleasant cause of Love, but the unpleasant cause of Hatred; he who is indifferent to them (*viz.* smells), is called dispassionate. (48)

The nose perceives "smell," and "smell" attracts the nose; the cause of Love is pleasant, and the cause of Hatred is unpleasant. (49)

He who is passionately fond of "smells," will come to untimely ruin; as an impassioned snake which is allured by the smell of a drug, when it comes out of its hole. (50)

He who passionately hates (a smell), will at the same moment suffer pain. It is the fault of an undisciplined man that he is annoyed (by a smell); it is not the "smell" itself that annoys him. (51)

He who is very fond of a lovely "smell," hates all others; hence a fool will suffer misery, but a dispassionate sage is not affected by it. (52)

He who has a passion for "smells," will kill many movable and immovable beings; a passionate fool, intent on his personal interest, pains and torments those beings in many ways. (53)

How can a man who passionately desires "smells," be happy while he gets, keeps, uses, loses, and misses (those things). Even when he enjoys them, he is never satisfied. (54)

When he is not satisfied with those "smells," and his craving for them grows stronger and stronger, he will become discontented, and unhappy by dint of his discontent; misled by greed he will take another's property. (55)

When he is overcome by violent desire, takes another's property, and is not satisfied with those "smells" and their possession, then his deceit and falsehood increase on account of his greed; yet he will not get rid of his misery. (56)

After and before he has lied, and when he is on the point of lying, he feels infinitely unhappy. Thus when he takes another's property, and is (after all) not satisfied by the "smells" (he has obtained), he becomes unhappy, and nobody will protect him. (57)

How, then, can a man who is devoted to "smells," ever derive any happiness from anything? He suffers pain at the time of their enjoyment to procure which he had suffered misery. (58)

In the same way he who hates "smells," incurs a long succession of pains; when his mind is filled with hatred, he accumulates Karman which in the end again produces misery. (59)

But a man who is indifferent to "smells," is free from sorrows; though still in the Saṃsāra, he is not affected by that long succession of pains, just as the leaf of the Lotus (is not moistened) by water. (60)

"Taste" attracts the tongue; it is the pleasant cause of Love, but the unpleasant cause of Hatred; he who is indifferent to them (*viz.* tastes), is called dispassionate. (61)

The tongue perceives "taste," and "taste" attracts the tongue; the cause of Love is pleasant, and the cause of Hatred is unpleasant. (62)

He who is passionately fond of "tastes," will come to untimely ruin; just as an impassioned fish which is eager to swallow the bait, has its body transfixed by a hook. (63)

He who passionately hates (a taste), will at the same moment suffer pain. It is the fault of an undisciplined man that he is annoyed (by a taste); it is not the "taste" itself that annoys him. (64)

He who is very fond of a lovely "taste," hates all others; hence a fool will suffer misery, but a dispassionate sage is not affected by it. (65)

He who has a passion for "tastes," will kill many movable and immovable beings; a passionate fool, intent on his personal interest, pains and torments those beings in many ways. (66)

How can a man who passionately desires "tastes," be happy while he gets, keeps, uses, loses, and misses (those things). Even when he enjoys them, he is never satisfied. (67)

When he is not satisfied with those "tastes," and his craving for them grows stronger and stronger, he will become discontented, and unhappy by dint of his discontent; misled by greed he will take another's property. (68)

When he is overcome by violent desire, takes another's property, and is not satisfied with those "tastes" and their possession, then his deceit and falsehood increase on account of his greed; yet he will not get rid of his misery. (69)

After and before he has lied, and when he is on the point of lying, he feels infinitely unhappy. Thus when he takes another's property, and is (after all) not satisfied by the "tastes" (he has obtained), he becomes unhappy, and nobody will protect him. (70)

How, then, can a man who is devoted to "tastes," ever derive any happiness from anything? He suffers pain at the time of their enjoyment to procure which he had suffered misery. (71)

In the same way he who hates "tastes," incurs a long succession of pains; when his mind is filled with hatred, he accumulates Karman which in the end again produces misery. (72)

But a man who is indifferent to "tastes," is free from sorrows; though still in the Saṃsāra, he is not affected by that long succession of pains, just as the leaf of the Lotus (is not moistened) by water. (73)

"Touch" attracts the body; it is the pleasant cause of Love, but the unpleasant cause of Hatred; he who is indifferent to them (*viz.* touchs), is called dispassionate. (74)

The body perceives "touch," and "touch" attracts the body; the cause of Love is pleasant, and the cause of Hatred is unpleasant. (75)

He who is passionately fond of "touch," will come to untimely ruin; just as an impassioned buffalo who dives in cold water, is taken hold of by a crocodile and dies. (76)

He who passionately hates (a touch), will at the same moment suffer pain. It is the fault of an undisciplined man that he is annoyed (by a touch); it is not the "touch" itself that annoys him. (77)

He who is very fond of a lovely "touch," hates all others; hence a fool will suffer misery, but a dispassionate sage is not affected by it. (78)

He who has a passion for "touchs," will kill many movable and immovable beings; a passionate fool, intent on his personal interest, pains and torments those beings in many ways. (79)

How can a man who passionately desires "touching," be happy while he gets, keeps, uses, loses, and misses (those things). Even when he enjoys them, he is never satisfied. (80)

When he is not satisfied with those "touches," and his craving for them grows stronger and stronger, he will become discontented, and unhappy by dint of his discontent; misled by greed he will take another's property. (81)

When he is overcome by violent desire, takes another's property, and is not satisfied with those "touches" and their possession, then his deceit and falsehood increase on account of his greed; yet he will not get rid of his misery. (82)

After and before he has lied, and when he is on the point of lying, he feels infinitely unhappy. Thus when he takes another's property, and is (after all) not satisfied by the "touches" (he has obtained), he becomes unhappy, and nobody will protect him. (83)

How, then, can a man who is devoted to "touch," ever derive any happiness from anything? He suffers pain at the time of their enjoyment to procure which he had suffered misery. (84)

In the same way he who hates "touch," incurs a long succession of pains; when his mind is filled with hatred, he accumulates Karman which in the end again produces misery. (85)

But a man who is indifferent to "touch," is free from sorrows; though still in the Saṃsāra, he is not affected by that long succession of pains, just as the leaf of the Lotus (is not moistened) by water. (86)

"Feeling" attracts the mind; it is the pleasant cause of Love, but the unpleasant cause of Hatred; he who is indifferent to them (*viz.* feelings), is called dispassionate. (87)

The mind perceives "feeling," and "feeling" attracts the mind; the cause of Love is pleasant, and the cause of Hatred is unpleasant. (88)

He who is passionately fond of "feelings," will come to untimely ruin; just as an impassioned elephant who is inflamed by carnal desires, is turned from his way by a female elephant (and is captured and at last killed in battle). (89)

He who passionately hates (a feeling), will at the same moment suffer pain. It is the fault of an undisciplined man that he is annoyed (by a feeling); it is not the "feeling" itself that annoys him. (90)

He who is very fond of a lovely "feeling," hates all others; hence a fool will suffer misery, but a dispassionate sage is not affected by it. (91)

He who has a passion for "feelings," will kill many movable and immovable beings; a passionate fool, intent on his personal interest, pains and torments those beings in many ways. (92)

How can a man who passionately desires "feelings," be happy while he gets, keeps, uses, loses, and misses (those things). Even when he enjoys them, he is never satisfied. (93)

When he is not satisfied with those "feelings," and his craving for them grows stronger and stronger, he will become discontented, and unhappy by dint of his discontent; misled by greed he will take another's property. (94)

When he is overcome by violent desire, takes anothers property, and is not satisfied with those "feelings" and their possession, then his deceit and falsehood increase on account of his greed; yet he will not get rid of his misery. (95)

After and before he has lied, and when he is on the point of lying, he feels infinitely unhappy. Thus when he takes anothers property, and is (after all) not satisfied by the "feelings" (he has obtained), he becomes unhappy, and nobody will protect him. (96)

How, then, can a man who is devoted to "feelings," ever derive any happiness from anything? He suffers pain at the time of their enjoyment to procure which he had suffered misery. (97)

In the same way he who hates "feelings," incurs a long succession of pains; when his mind is filled with hatred, he accumulates Karman which in the end again produces misery. (98)

But a man who is indifferent to "feelings," is free from sorrows; though still in the Saṃsāra, he is not affected by that long succession of pains, just as the leaf of the Lotus (is not moistened) by water. (99)

Thus the objects of the senses and of the mind cause pain to passionate men, but they never in the least cause any pain to the dispassionate. (100)

Pleasant things (by themselves) do not cause indifference nor emotions (as anger, etc.); but by either hating or loving them, a man undergoes such a change through delusion. (101)

Anger, pride, deceit, greed; disgust, aversion to self-control and delight in sensual things;[17] mirth, fear, sorrow, carnal desire for women, men, or both; all these manifold passions arise in him who is attached to pleasures; and so do other emotions produced by those (before mentioned) arise in him who is to be pitied, who (ought to be) ashamed of himself, and who is hateful. (102, 103)

A monk should not desire a companion, not (even) one who is able to perform his religious duties; nor, if he regrets having taken the vows, (should he desire for) a worldly reward of his austerities.[18] Such emotions of an infinite variety arise in one who is the slave of his senses. (104)

Desiring happiness and being submerged in the ocean of delusion, he forms many plans for warding off misery; and for their sake an impassioned man exerts himself. (105)

But all kinds of objects of the senses, sounds, etc., will cause to the indifferent neither a pleasant nor an unpleasant feeling. (106)

He who endeavours to recognise the vanity of all desires,[19] will arrive at perfect indifference. When he ceases to desire the objects (of the senses), his desire for pleasures will become extinct. (107)

The dispassionate man who has performed all duties will quickly remove the obstructions to right knowledge and to right faith, and whatever Karman produces obstruction (to righteousness). (108)

Then he knows and sees all things, he is free from delusion and hindrances, his āsravas have gone, and he is proficient in meditation and concentration of thoughts, and being pure he will arrive at beatitude when his life is spent. (109)

He will get rid of all misery which always afflicts mankind; recovered from the long illness, as it were, and glorious, he becomes infinitely happy, and obtains the (final) aim. (110)

We have taught the way how to become exempt from all misery which arises since time without beginning; those beings who follow it will in their time become infinitely happy. (111)

Thus I say.

Thirty-Third Lecture: The Nature of Karman

I shall now in due order explain the eight kinds of Karman, bound by which the soul turns round and round in the Circle of Births. (1)

The eight kinds of Karman are briefly the following:

1. Jñānāvaraṇīya (which acts as an obstruction to right knowledge);

2. Darśanāvaraṇīya (which acts as an obstruction to right faith);

3. Vēdanīya (which leads to experiencing pain or pleasure);

4. Mōhanīya (which leads to delusion);

5. Āyuḥkarman (which determines the length of life);

6. Nāman (which determines the name or individuality of the embodied soul);

7. Gōtra (which determines his Gōtra);

8. Antarāya (which prevents ones entrance on the path that leads to eternal bliss).[1] (2, 3)

1. Obstruction of knowledge is fivefold (*viz.* obstruction to):

a. Śruta, knowledge derived from the sacred books;

b. Ābhinibōdhika, perception;

c. Avadhijñāna, supernatural knowledge;

d. Manaḥparyāya, knowledge of the thoughts of other people;

e. Kēvala, the highest, unlimited knowledge. (4)

2. The nine kinds of obstruction to right faith are: 1. sleep; 2. activity; 3. very deep sleep; 4. a high degree of activity;[2] 5. a state of deep-rooted greed; 6-9 refer to faith in the objects of the first three and the last kinds of knowledge. (5, 6)

3. Vēdanīya is twofold, pleasure and pain; there are many subdivisions of pleasure and so there are of pain also. (7)

4. Mōhanīya is twofold as referring to faith and to conduct; the first is threefold, the second twofold. (8)

The three kinds of Mōhanīya referring to faith are: 1. right faith; 2. wrong faith; 3. faith partly right and partly wrong. (9)

The two kinds of Mōhanīya referring to conduct are: 1. what is experienced in the form of the four cardinal passions; 2. what is experienced in the form of feelings different from them. (10)

The first kind of this Karman is sixteenfold, the second sevenfold or ninefold.[3] (11)

5. Āyuṣka is fourfold as referring to 1. denizens of hell; 2. brute creation; 3. men; 4. gods. (12)

6. Nāman is twofold, good and bad; there are many subdivisions of the good variety, and so there are of the bad one also.[4] (13)

7. Gōtra is twofold, high and low; the first is eightfold, and so is the second also. (14)

8. Antarāya is fivefold as preventing: 1. gifts; 2. profit; 3. momentary enjoyment; 4. continuous enjoyment;[5] and 5. power. (15)

Thus the division of Karman and the subdivisions have been told.

Now hear their number of atoms,[6] place, time, and development. (16)

The number of atoms of every Karman is infinite; it is (infinitely) greater than (the number) of fettered[7] souls, but less than that of the perfected ones. (17)

The Karman in the six directions of space[8] binds all souls, and it binds the whole soul in all its parts in every possible way. (18)

The longest duration (of Karman) is thirty Krores of Krores of Sāgarōpamās,[9] and the ṣortest a part of a muhūrta. (19)

This holds good with both āvaraṇīyas, with Vēdanīya and Antarāya. (20)

The longest duration of Mōhanīya is seventy Krores of Krores of Sāgarōpamās, and the shortest a part of a muhūrta. (21)

The longest duration of āyuṣka is thirty-three Krores of Krores of Sāgarōpamās, and the shortest a part of a muhūrta. (22)

The longest duration of Nāman and Gōtra is twenty Krores of

Krores of Sāgarōpamās, and the shortest eight muhūrtas. (23)

The number of perfected souls is infinite, and that of the subdivisions of Karman[10] is also (infinite); the number of atoms in all these (subdivisions) exceeds (the number) of all souls. (24)

Therefore a wise man should know the different subdivisions of these Karmans, and should exert himself to prevent and to destroy them. (25)

Thus I say.

Thirty-Fourth Lecture: On Lēsyā [1]

I shall deliver in due order the Lecture on Lēśyā; hear the nature of the six Lēśyās (produced by) Karman. (1)

Hear 1. the names, 2. colours, 3. tastes, 4. smells, 5. touches, 6. degrees, 7. character, 8. variety, 9. duration, 10. result, and 11. life of the Lēśyās. (2)

1. They are named in the following order: black, blue, grey, red, yellow, and white. (3)

2. The black Lēśyā has the colour of a rain-cloud, a buffalos horn, (the fruit of) Riṣṭaka,[2] or the eye of the wagtail. (4)

The blue Lēśyā has the colour of the blue Aśōka,[3] the tail of the Chaṣa,[4] or of lapis lazuli. (5)

The grey Lēśyā has the colour of the flower of Atasī,[5] the feathers of the Kōkila, or the collar of pigeons. (6)

The red Lēśyā has the colour of vermilion, the rising sun, or the bill of a parrot. (7)

The yellow Lēśyā has the colour of orpiment, turmeric, or the flowers of Śaṇa[6] and Asana.[7] (8)

The white Lēśyā has the colour of a conch-shell, the aṅka-stone,[8] Kunda-flowers,[9] flowing milk, silver, or a necklace of pearls. (9)

3. The taste of the black Lēśyā is infinitely more bitter than that of Tumbaka,[10] (the fruit of the) Nimb-tree,[11] or of Rōhiṇī. (10)

The taste of the blue Lēśyā is infinitely more pungent than Trikaṭuka[12] and Hastipippalī. (11)

The taste of grey Lēśyā is infinitely sourer than that of unripe

Mango and Kapittha.[13] (12)

The taste of red Lēśyā is infinitely more pleasant than that of ripe Mango and Kapittha. (13)

The taste of yellow Lēśyā is infinitely better than that of excellent wine and various liquors, honey and Mairēyaka.[14] (14)

The taste of white Lēśyā is infinitely better than that of dates, grapes, milk, candied and pounded sugar. (15)

The smell of the bad Lēśyās (*viz.* the three first) is infinitely worse than that of the corpse of a cow, dog, or snake. (16)

The smell of the three good Lēśyās is infinitely more pleasant than that of fragrant flowers and of perfumes when they are pounded. (17)

5. The touch of the bad Lēśyās is infinitely worse than that of a saw, the tongue of a cow, or leaf of the Teak tree. (18)

The touch of the three good Lēśyās is infinitely more pleasant than that of cotton, butter, or Śirīṣa-flowers.[15] (19)

6. The degrees[16] of the Lēśyās are three, or nine, or twenty-seven, or eighty-one, or two hundred and forty-three. (20)

7. A man who acts on the impulse of the five āsravas,[17] does not possess the three Guptis, has not ceased to injure the six (kinds of living beings), commits cruel acts, is wicked and violent, is afraid of no consequences,[18] is mischievous and does not subdue his senses—a man of such habits develops the black Lēśyā. (21, 22)

A man of the following qualities: envy, anger, want of self-control, ignorance, deceit, want of modesty, greed, hatred, wickedness, carelessness, love of enjoyment; a man who pursues pleasures and does not abstain from sinful undertakings, who is wicked and violent—a man of such habits develops the blue Lēśyā. (23, 24)

A man who is dishonest in words and acts, who is base, not upright, a dissembler and deceiver,[19] a heretic, a vile man, a talker of hurtful and sinful things, a thief, and full of jealousy—a man of such habits develops the grey Lēśyā. (25, 26)

A man who is humble, steadfast, free from deceit and inquisitiveness, well disciplined, restrained, attentive to his study and duties,[20] who loves the Law and keeps it, who is afraid of forbidden things and strives after the highest good—a man of such habits develops the red Lēśyā. (27, 28)

A man who has but little anger, pride, deceit, and greed, whose mind is at ease, who controls himself, who is attentive to his study and duties, who speaks but little, is calm, and subdues his senses—a man of such habits develops the yellow Lēśyā. (29, 30)

A man who abstains from constant thinking about his misery and about sinful deeds, but engages in meditation on the Law and truth only,[21] whose mind is at ease, who controls himself, who practises the Samitis and Guptis, whether he be still subject to passion or free from passion, is calm, and subdues his senses—a man of such habits develops the white Lēśyā. (31, 32)

8. There are as many varieties[22] of Lēśyās as there are Samayas[23] in the innumerable Avasarpiṇīs and Utsarpiṇīs, and as there are countless worlds. (33)

9. Half a muhūrta is the shortest, and thirty-three Sāgarōpamās plus one muhūrta is the longest duration of the black Lēśyā. (34)

Half a muhūrta is the shortest, and ten Sāgarōpamās plus one Palyōpamā and a part of an Asaṃkhyēya is the longest duration of the blue Lēśyā. (35)

Half a muhūrta is the shortest, and three Sāgarōpamās plus one Palyōpamā and a part of an Asaṃkhyēya is the longest duration of the grey Lēśyā. (36)

Half a muhūrta is the shortest, and two Sāgarōpamās plus one Palyōpamā and a part of an Asaṃkhyēya is the longest duration of the red Lēśyā. (37)

Half a muhūrta is the shortest, and ten Sāgarōpamās plus one muhūrta is the longest duration of the yellow Lēśyā. (38)

Half a muhūrta is the shortest, and thirty-three Sāgarōpamās plus one muhūrta is the longest duration of the white Lēśyā. (39)

I have described above the duration of the Lēśyās generally; I shall now detail their duration in the four walks of mundane existence.[24] (40)

The shortest duration of the grey Lēśyā (of a denizen of hell) is ten thousand years, the longest three Sāgarōpamās plus one Palyōpamā and part of an Asaṃkhyēya. (41)

The shortest duration of the blue Lēśyā (of a denizen of hell) is three Sāgarōpamās plus one Palyōpamā and a part of an Asaṃkhyēya, the longest ten Sāgarōpamās plus one Palyōpamā and a part of an Asaṃkhyēya. (42)

The shortest duration of the black Lēśyā (of a denizen of hell) is ten Sāgarōpamās plus one Palyōpamā and a part of an Asaṃkhyēya, the longest thirty-three Sāgarōpamās. (43)

I have described the duration of the Lēśyās of denizens of hell; I shall now describe that of animals, men, and gods. (44)

The duration of any of the Lēśyās except the best (*viz.* white one) is less than a muhūrta for (the lowest organisms), animals, and men.[25] (45)

Half a muhūrta is the shortest duration of the white Lēśyā (of animals and men), and the longest a Krore of former years[26] less nine years. (46)

I have described the duration of the Lēśyās of animals and men, I shall now describe that of the gods. (47)

The shortest duration of the black Lēśyā is ten thousand years, the longest a Palyōpamā and (a part of) an Asaṃkhyēya. (48)

The shortest duration of the blue Lēśyā is equal to the longest of the black one plus one Samaya; the longest is one Palyōpamā plus a (greater part of) an Asaṃkhyēya. (49)

The shortest duration of the grey Lēśyā is equal to the longest of the blue one plus one Samaya; the longest is one Palyōpamā plus (a still greater part of) an Asaṃkhyēya. (50)

I shall now describe the red Lēśyā as it is with gods, Bhavanapatis, Vyantaras, Jyōtiṣkas, and Vaimānikas. (51)

The shortest duration of the red Lēśyā is one Palyōpamā, the longest two Sāgarōpamās plus one Palyōpamā and a part of an Asaṃkhyēya.[27] (52)

The shortest duration of the red Lēśyā is ten thousand years, the longest two Sāgarōpamās plus one Palyōpamā and a part of an Asaṃkhyēya. (53)

The longest duration of the red Lēśyā plus one Samaya is equal to the shortest of the yellow Lēśyā; its longest, however, is ten muhūrtas longer. (54)

The longest duration of the yellow Lēśyā plus one Samaya is equal to the shortest of the white Lēśyā; the longest, however, is thirty-three muhūrtas longer. (55)

10. The black, blue, and grey Lēśyās are the lowest Lēśyās; through them the soul is brought into miserable courses of life. (56)

The red, yellow, and white Lēśyās are the good Lēśyās; through them the soul is brought into happy courses of life. (57)

11. In the first moment of these Lēśyās when they are joined (with the soul), the latter is not born into a new existence.[28] (58)

In the last moment of all these Lēśyās when they are joined (with the soul), the latter is not born into a new existence. (59)

While the last muhūrta is running and a part of it is still to come, the souls with their Lēśyās developed, go to a new birth. (60)

A wise man should, therefore, know the nature of these Lēśyās; he should avoid the bad ones and obtain the good ones. (61)

Thus I say.

Thirty-Fifth Lecture: The Houseless Monk

Learn from me, with attentive minds, the road shown by the wise ones,[1] which leads a monk who follows it, to the end of all misery. (1)

Giving up the life in a house, and taking Pravrajyā, a sage should know and renounce those attachments which take hold of men. (2)

A restrained monk should abstain from killing, lying, stealing, carnal intercourse, from desire, love, and greed. (3)

Even in his thoughts a monk should not long for a pleasant painted house filled with the fragrance of garlands and frankincense, secured by doors, and decorated with a white ceiling-cloth.[2] (4)

For in such a dwelling a monk will find it difficult to prevent his senses from increased desire and passion. (5)

He should be content to live on a burial-place, in a deserted house, below a tree, in solitude, or in a place which had been prepared for the sake of somebody else.[3] (6)

A well-controlled monk should live in a pure place, which is not too much crowded, and where no women live. (7)

He should not build a house, nor cause others to erect one; for many living beings both movable and immovable, both subtile and gross, are seen to be killed when a house is being built; therefore a monk should abstain from building a house. (8, 9)

The same holds good with the cooking of food and drink, or with ones causing them to be cooked. Out of compassion for living beings one should not cook nor cause another to cook. (10)

Beings which live in water, corn, or in earth and wood, are

destroyed in food and drink; therefore a monk should cause nobody to cook. (11)

There is nothing so dangerous as fire, for it spreads in all directions and is able to destroy many beings; one should therefore not light a fire. (12)

Even in his thoughts a monk should not long for gold and silver; indifferent alike to dirt and gold he abstains from buying and selling. (13)

If he buys, he becomes a buyer; if he sells, he becomes a merchant; a monk is not to engage in buying and selling. (14)

A monk who is to live on alms, should beg and not buy; buying and selling is a great sin; but to live on alms is benefitting. (15)

He should collect his alms in small parts according to the Sūtras and so as to avoid faults; a monk should contentedly go on his begging-tour, whether he get alms or not. (16)

A great sage should not eat for the sake of the pleasant taste (of the food) but for the sustenance of life, being not dainty nor eager for good fare, restraining his tongue, and being without cupidity. (17)

Even in his thoughts he should not desire to be presented with flowers, to be offered a seat, to be eloquently greeted, or to be offered presents, or to get a magnificent welcome and treatment. (18)

He should meditate on true things only,[4] committing no sins and having no property; he should walk about careless of his body till his end arrives. (19)

Rejecting food when the time of his death arrives, and leaving the human body, he becomes his own master,[5] and is liberated from misery. (20)

Without property, without egoism, free from passions and the āsravas, he obtains absolute knowledge, and reaches eternal beatitude. (21)

Thus I say.

Thirty-Sixth Lecture: On Living Beings and Things Without Life [1]

Now learn from me with attentive minds the division of Living Beings and Things without life,[2] which a monk must know who is to exert himself in self-control. (1)

The Living Beings and the Things without life make up this world (Lōka); but the space where only Things without life are found is called the Non-world (Alōka). (2)

The Living Beings and the Things without life will be described with reference to 1. substance, 2. place, 3. time, and 4. development. (3)

A. Things without life.

Things without life are 1. possessing form, 2. formless; the formless things are of ten kinds, those possessing form are of four kinds. (4)

(1) The ten kinds of formless things: 1. Dharma, 2. its divisions, 3. its indivisible parts; 4. Adharma, 5. its divisions, 6. its indivisible parts; 7. space, 8. its divisions, 9. its indivisible parts, and 10. time.[3] (5, 6)

Dharma and Adharma are co-extensive with the World (Lōka); space fills the World and the Non-world (Alōka); time exists in what is called the place of time.[4] (7)

Dharma, Adharma, and Space are ever without beginning and end. (8)

And time also, if regarded as a continuous flow,[5] is called so (*i.e.* without beginning and end); but with regard to an individual thing it has a beginning and an end. (9)

(2) The four kinds of things possessing form are 1. compound things,

2. their divisions, 3. their indivisible parts, and 4. atoms.[6] (10)

Compound things and atoms occur as individual things and apart (or different from others),[7] in the whole world and in parts of the world; this is their distribution with regard to place. (11)

Subtile things occur all over the world, gross things only in a part of it.

I shall now give their fourfold division with regard to time. (12)

With regard to the continuous flow (or development of a thing) it is without beginning and without end; but with regard to its existence (as an individual thing) it has both a beginning and an end.[8] (13)

The longest duration of Things without life possessing form is an immeasurable[9] period; the shortest one Samaya. (14)

The longest interruption[10] in the existence of Things without life possessing form is an endless time; the shortest one Samaya. (15)

Their development is fivefold: with regard to 1. colour, 2. smell, 3. taste, 4. touch, and 5. figure. (16)

Those which develop with regard to colour are of five kinds: 1. black, 2. blue, 3. red, 4. yellow, 5. white. (17)

Those which develop with regard to smell are of two kinds: 1. sweet-smelling substances, and 2. of bad smell. (18)

Those which develop with regard to taste are of five kinds: 1. bitter, 2. pungent, 3. astringent, 4. sour, and 5. sweet. (19)

Those which develop with regard to touch are of eight kinds: 1. hard, 2. soft, 3. heavy, 4. light, 5. cold, 6. hot, 7. smooth, and 8. rough.

In this way the substances have been declared, which develop with regard to touch. (20, 21)

Those which develop with regard to figure are of five kinds: 1. globular, 2. circular, 3. triangular, 4. square, and 5. long. (22)

Things of black colour are subdivided with regard to smell, taste, touch, and figure. (23)

The same subdivision holds good with blue, red, yellow, and white things. (24-27 [11])

Things of sweet smell are subdivided with regard to colour, taste, touch, and figure; things of bad smell are similarly subdivided. (28, 29)

Things of bitter taste are subdivided with regard to colour, smell, touch, and figure. (30)

The same subdivision holds good with pungent, astringent, sour, and sweet things. (31-34)

Things of hard touch are subdivided with regard to colour, smell, taste, and figure. (35)

The same subdivision holds good with soft, heavy, light, cold, hot, smooth, and rough things. (36-42)

Things of globular figure are subdivided with regard to colour, smell, taste, and touch. (43)

The same subdivision holds good with circular, triangular, square, and long things. (44-47)

Thus the division of Things without life has briefly been told.

B. Living Beings.

I shall now, in due order, deliver the division of living beings. (48)

Living beings are of two kinds: 1. those still belonging to the Saṃsāra, and 2. the perfected souls (siddhas). The latter are of many kinds; hear me explain them. (49)

(1) The perfected souls are those of women, men, hermaphrodites, of orthodox, heterodox, and householders. (50)

Perfection is reached by people of the greatest, smallest, and middle size,[12] on high places, underground, on the surface of the earth, in the ocean, and in water (of rivers, etc.). (51)

Ten hermaphrodites reach, at the same time, perfection, twenty women, one hundred and eight men; four householders, ten heterodox, and one hundred and eight orthodox monks. (52, 53)

Two individuals of the greatest size reach perfection (simultaneously), four of the smallest size, and one hundred and eight of the middle size. (54)

Four individuals reach perfection (simultaneously) on high places, two in the ocean, three in water, twenty underground, and one hundred and eight on the surface of the earth. (55)

From where are the perfected souls debarred? Where do the perfected souls reside? Where do they leave their bodies, and where do they go, on reaching perfection? (56)

Perfected souls are debarred from the non-world (Alōka); they reside on the top of the world; they leave their bodies here (below), and go there, on reaching perfection. (57)

Twelve Yōjanas above the (Vimāna) Sarvārtha is the place called Īṣatprāgbhāra,[13] which has the form of an umbrella; (there the perfected souls go). (58)

It is forty-five hundred thousand Yōjanas long, and as many broad, and it is somewhat more than three times as many in circumference. (59)

Its thickness is eight Yōjanas, it is greatest in the middle, and decreases[14] toward the margin, till it is thinner than the wing of a fly. (60)

This place, by nature pure, consisting of white gold, resembles in form an open umbrella, as has been said by the best of Jinas. (61)

(Above it) is a pure blessed place (called Śītā), which is white like a conch-shell, the aṅka-stone,[15] and Kunda-flowers; a Yōjana thence is the end of the world. (62)

The perfected souls penetrate the sixth part[16] of the uppermost Krōśa of the (above-mentioned) Yōjana. (63)

There at the top of the world reside the blessed perfected souls, rid of all transmigration, and arrived at the excellent state of perfection. (64)

The dimension of a perfected soul is two-thirds of the height which the individual had in his last existence. (65)

The perfected souls, considered singly, (as individuals) have a beginning but no end; considered collectively[17] (as a class) they have neither a beginning nor an end. (66)

They have no (visible) form, they consist of Life throughout, they are developed into knowledge and, faith, and they possess paramount happiness which admits of no comparison. (67)

They all dwell in one part of the world, and have developed into knowledge and faith, they have crossed the boundary of the Saṃsāra, and reached the excellent state of perfection. (68)

(2) Living beings which still belong to the Saṃsāra, are of two kinds: a. movable, and b. immovable ones: the immovable ones are of three kinds: (69)

α. Earth Lives, β. Water Lives, and γ. plants; these are the three kinds of immovable living beings; now learn from me their subdivision. (70)

α. The Earth Lives are of two kinds: subtile and gross; and both of them are either fully developed or undeveloped. (71)

The gross and fully developed are of two kinds: *viz.* smooth or rough. The smooth ones are of seven kinds: (72)

Black, blue, red, yellow, white, pale dust, and clay.

The rough ones are of thirty-six kinds: (73)

Earth, gravel, sand, stones, rocks, rock-salt,[18] iron, copper, tin, lead, silver, gold, and diamond; (74)

Orpiment, vermilion, realgar, Sāsaka,[19] antimony, coral, Abhrapaṭala, Abhravāluka; these are varieties of gross (Earth-) bodies and kinds of precious stones. (75)

Hyacinth, natron, Aṅka, crystal, Lōhitākṣa, emerald, Masāragalla, Bhujamōchaka, and sapphire; (76)

Chandana, red chalk, Haṃsagarbha, Pulaka,[20] and sulphur; Chandraprabha, lapis lazuli, Jalakānta, and Sūryakānta.[21] (77)

These thirty-six kinds of "rough earth" have been enumerated. The "subtile earth" is but of one kind, as there is no variety. (78)

The subtile species is distributed all over the world, but the gross one (is found) in a part of the world only.

I shall now give their fourfold division with regard to time. (79)

With regard to the continuous flow (or development of an earth-body) it is without a beginning and end; but with regard to its existence in its present form it has both a beginning and end. (80)

Twenty-two thousand years is the longest duration of the Earth Lives; its shortest is less than a muhūrta. (81)

The longest duration of the body of Earth Lives, if they do not leave that (kind of) body,[22] is an immeasurable time; the shortest is less than one muhūrta. (82)

The longest interval between an Earth Lives leaving its body (till its return to it), is an endless time; the shortest less than one Muhūrta. (83)

Their varieties, caused by (difference of) colour, smell, taste, touch, figure, and place, are (counted) by thousands. (84)

β. The Water Lives are of two kinds: subtile and gross ones; and both of them are either fully developed or undeveloped. (85)

The gross and fully developed ones are of five kinds: pure water, dew, exudations, fog, and ice. (86)

The "subtile water" is of one kind, as there is no variety. The subtile species is distributed all over the world, but the gross one (is found) in a part of the world only. (87)

With regard to the continuous flow, etc. (as in verse 80).

Seven thousand years is the longest duration of the life of Water Lives, etc. (as in verse 81). (All that has been said of Earth Lives in verses 82-84 is verbally repeated here of "Water Lives.") (88-92)

γ. Plants are of two kinds: subtile and gross ones; and both of them are either fully developed or undeveloped. (93)

The gross and fully developed plants are of two kinds: either many have one body in common, or each has its own body. (94)

Those who severally have their own body are of many kinds: trees, shrubby plants,[23] shrubs,[24] big plants,[25] creeping plants,[26] grass;[27] (95)

Palms,[28] plants of knotty stems or stalks,[29] mushrooms,[30] water-plants, annual plants,[31] and herbs.[32] These are called plants possessing severally their own body. (96)

Those plants of which many have one body in common are of many kinds:[33] Āluya,[34] Mūlaya,[35] ginger; (97)

Harilī, Sirilī, Sassirilī, Jāvaī, Kēyakandalī,[36] onion, garlic, plantain-tree, Kuḍuvvaya;[37] (98)

Lōhiṇīhūya, Thīhūya, Tuhaga, Kaṇha,[38] Vajjakanda,[39] Sūraṇaya;[40] (99)

Assakaṇṇī,[41] Sīhakaṇṇī, Musuṇḍhī, turmeric, and many others besides. (100)

The subtile plants are of one kind, as there is no variety. Subtile plants are distributed all over the world, gross plants (are found) in a part of the world only. (101)

With regard to the continuous flow, etc. (as in verse 80). (102)

Ten thousand years is the longest duration of the life of plants, etc. (All as in verses 81-84. Substitute plants, which are here called vanaspati and panaka, for Earth-bodies.) (103-106)

Thus the three kinds of immovable living beings have briefly been told. I shall now explain in due order the three kinds of movable living beings. (107)

b. The movable beings are α. the Fire Lives, α. the Wind Lives, and γ. those with an organic body; these are the three kinds of movable beings. Learn from me their subdivision. (108)

α. The Fire Lives are of two kinds: subtile and gross ones; and both of them are either fully developed or undeveloped. (109)

The gross and fully developed ones are of many kinds: coal, burning chaff, fire, and flame of fire; (110)

Meteors, and lightning, and many other kinds besides.

The subtile Fire Lives are but of one kind, as there is no variety. (111)

The subtile species, etc. (see verses 79-84. Substitute Fire Lives for Earth Lives. In verses 114 f., corresponding to verses 81, 89, and 103, read: "the longest duration of the life of Fire Lives is three days," etc.; the rest as above). (112-117)

β. The Wind Lives are of two kinds, etc. (as in verse 109). (118)

The gross and fully developed ones are of five kinds: squalls,[42] whirlwinds,[43] thick winds,[44] high winds, low winds; (119)

And the Saṃvartaka[45] wind, etc.; thus they are of many kinds.[46]

The subtile Wind Lives are but of one kind, as there is no variety. (120)

The subtile species, etc. (as above 79-84. Substitute Wind Lives for Earth Lives. In verse 123, corresponding to 114, read: "the longest duration of the life of Wind Lives is three thousand years"; the rest as above). (121-126)

γ. Movable beings with organic bodies (*i.e.* animals) are of four kinds: i. those possessing two organs of sense, ii. those with three organs, iii. those with four organs, iv. those with five organs. (127)

i. Beings with two organs of sense are of two kinds: subtile and gross ones. Both are either fully developed or undeveloped. Learn from me their subdivision.[47] (128)

Worms, Sōmaṅgala, Alasa,[48] Māivāhaya,[49] Vāsīmuha,[50] shells, conches, Saṅkhāṇaga;[51] (129)

Pallōya, Aṇullaya, cowries, leeches, Jālaga, and Chandaṇa.[52] (130)

These and others are the many kinds of beings with two organs of sense. All of them live in a part of the world only, they do not live everywhere. (131)

With regard to the continuous flow, etc. (as in verse 80). (132)

The duration of the life of beings with two organs of sense is twelve years at the utmost; the shortest is less than a muhūrta. (133)

The longest duration of the body of beings with two organs of sense is a Saṃkhyēya (or measurable time) if they do not leave that (kind of) body; the shortest is less than one muhūrta. (134)

135, 136 = 83, 84. Substitute "beings with two organs of sense" for Earth Lives.

ii. Beings with three organs of sense are of two kinds: subtile and gross ones. Both are either fully developed or undeveloped. Learn from me their subdivision. (137)

Kunthu,[53] ants, bugs, Ukkala, white ants, Taṇahāra, Kaṭṭhahāra, Mālūga,[54] Pattahāraga; (138)

Duga shining like lead, which originate in the kernel of the cotton-seed, Sadāvarī, centipedes, Indagāiya; (139)

Cochineal, etc. Thus they are of many kinds. All of them live in a part of the world only, they do not live everywhere. (140)

141-145 = 132-136. (Substitute "beings with three organs of sense." The longest duration, etc., is forty-nine days, verse 142 = 133.)

iii. Beings with four organs of sense are of two kinds: subtile and gross ones. Both are either developed or undeveloped. Learn from me their subdivision. (146)

Andhiya, Pottiyā, flies, mosquitoes, bees, moths, Dhiṅkaṇa and Kaṅkaṇa; (147)

Kukkuḍa,[55] Siṅgirīḍī, Nandāvatta,[56] scorpions, Ḍōla, crickets, Viralī, Acchivēhaya; (148)

Acchila, Sāhaya Acchirōdaya, Vichitta, Vichittapattaya,[57] Uhilṃjaliyā, Jalakārī, Nīyā, and Tantavagāiyā. (149)

These and others are the beings with four organs of sense. All of them, etc. (the rest as in verses 131-136. Substitute "beings with four organs of sense." The longest duration, etc., is six months, verse 152 = 133). (150-155)

iv. Beings with five organs of sense are of four kinds: denizens of hell, animals,[58] men, and gods. (156).

a. Denizens of hell are of seven kinds according to the seven hells; they are called Ratnābha, Śarkarābha, Vālukābha; (157)

Paṅkābha, Dhūmābha, Tamā, and Tamatamā. Thus the seven kinds of denizens of hell have been enumerated. (158)

All the (denizens of hell) live in a part of the world only; they do not live everywhere, etc. (as in verses 79 and 80). (159, 160)

In the first hell the longest duration of their life is one Sāgarōpamā; the shortest is ten thousand years. (161)

In the second hell the longest duration of their life is three Sāgarōpamās; the shortest is one Sāgarōpamā.[59] (162)

In the third hell the longest duration of their life is seven Sāgarōpamās; the shortest is three Sāgarōpamās. (163)

In the fourth hell the longest duration of their life is ten Sāgarōpamās; the shortest is seven Sāgarōpamās. (164)

In the fifth hell the longest duration of their life is seventeen Sāgarōpamās; the shortest is ten Sāgarōpamās. (165)

In the sixth hell the longest duration of their life is twenty-two Sāgarōpamās; the shortest is seventeen Sāgarōpamās. (166)

In the seventh hell the longest duration of their life is thirty-three Sāgarōpamās; the shortest is twenty-two Sāgarōpamās. (167)

The length of the life of denizens of hell is also that of their continuance in the same kind of body, with regard both to the longest and shortest duration of it. (168)

Verses 169, 170 = 83, 84. (Substitute, denizens of hell.)

b. The animals which possess five organs of sense are of two kinds, those which originate by generatio aequivoca,[60] and those which are born from the womb. (171)

Either of them are again of three kinds: 1. aquatic, 2. terrestrial, and 3. aerial animals. Learn from me their subdivision. (172)

1. Fishes, tortoises, crocodiles, Makaras, and Gangetic porpoises are the five kinds of aquatic animals. (173)

174, 175 = 159, 160.

The longest duration of the life of aquatic animals is one Krore of former years;[61] the shortest is less than one muhūrta. (176)

The longest duration of the aquatic animals' continuance in the (same kind of body) is from two to nine[62] Krores of former years. (177)

178 = 83.

2. Quadrupeds and reptiles are the two kinds of terrestrial animals. The quadrupeds are of four kinds; listen to my description of them: (179)

(1) Solidungular animals, as horses, etc.;

(2) Biungular animals, as cows, etc.;

(3) Multiungular animals, as elephants, etc.;

(4) Animals having toes with nails, as lions, etc. (180)

The reptiles are of two kinds: 1. those which walk on their arms, as lizards, etc., and 2. those which move on their breast, as snakes, etc. Both are again of many kinds. (181)

182, 183 = 159, 160.

The longest duration of the life of terrestrial animals is three Palyōpamās; the shortest is less than one muhūrta. (184)

The longest duration of the terrestrial animals' continuance in the (same kind of) body is three Palyōpamās plus from two to nine Krores of former years; the shortest is less than one muhūrta. (185)

186 = 83.

3. Winged animals are of four kinds: those with membranous wings,[63] those with feathered wings, those with wings in the shape of a box,[64] and those (which sit on) outspread wings.[65] (187)

188, 189 = 159, 160.

The longest duration of the life of aerial animals is an Asaṃkhyēya-part of a Palyōpamā;[66] the shortest is less than one muhūrta. (190)

The longest duration (of the aerial animals' continuance in the same kind of body) is an Asaṃkhyēya-part of a Palyōpamā plus from two to nine Krores of former years; the shortest is less than one muhūrta. (191)

192, 193 = 159, 160.

c. Men are of two kinds; listen to my description of them: men originating by generatio aequivoca,[67] and men born from the womb. (194)

Those who are born from the womb are of three kinds: those living in the Karmabhūmi,[68] those living in the Akarmabhūmi, and those living on the minor continents.[69] (195)

They have, in the same order, fifteen,[70] thirty,[71] and twenty-eight subdivisions. These are the numbers handed down. (196)

Men originating by generatio aequivoca are of as many kinds. They all live but in a part of the world. (197)

Verses 198-202 = 183-186. (Substitute, "men" for "terrestrial animals.")

d. Gods are of four kinds; listen to my description of them: 1. Bhaumēyikas; 2. Vyantaras; 3. Jyōtiṣkas; 4. Vaimānikas. (203)

There are ten kinds of Bhavanavāsins (= Bhaumēyikas), eight of those who live in woods (= Vyantaras), five of Jyōtiṣkas, and two of Vaimānikas. (204)

1. The Bhavanavāsins are: the Asura-, Nāga-, Suvarṇa-, Vidyut-, Agni-, Dvīpa-, Udadhi-, Vāta-, and Ghaṇika-(Kumāras[72]). (2(15)

2. The eight kinds of Vyantaras are: Piśāchas, 3. The moons, the suns, the Nakṣatras, the planets, and the hosts of stars are the fivefold dwellings of the Jyōtiṣkas. (207)

4. The Vaimānika gods are of two kinds: *a'*. those who are born in the heavenly Kalpas, and *b'*. those who are born in the regions above them.[73] (208)

a'. The former are of twelve kinds: those who live in (the following Kalpas, after which they are named): Saudharma, Īśāna, Sanatkumāra, Māhēndra, Brahmalōka, and Lantaka; (209)

Mahāśukla, Sahasrāra, ānata, Prāṇata,[74] āraṇa, and Achyuta. These are the gods who are born in Kalpas. (210)

b'. The gods who are born in the regions above the Kalpas are of two kinds: α'. the Graivēyakas,[75] and β'. the Anuttaras.[76] The Graivēyakas are of nine kinds. (211)

α'. The lowest of the lowest, the middle of the lowest, the highest of the lowest, the lowest of the middle; (212)

The middle of the middle, the highest of the middle, the lowest of the highest, the middle of the highest; (213)

The highest of the highest. These are the Graivēyaka gods.

β'. The Vijayas, the Vaijayantas, the Jayantas, the Aparājitas (214)

And the Sarvārthasiddhas: these are the five kinds of Anuttara gods.

These and others besides are the many kinds of Vaimānika gods. (215-217 = 159-160)

The longest duration of the life of the Bhaumēyika gods is

somewhat more than a Sāgarōpamā, the smallest ten thousand years. (218)

The longest duration of the life of the Vyantaras is one Palyōpamā, the shortest is ten thousand years. (219)

The longest duration of the life of the Jyōtiṣkas is one Palyōpamā plus one hundred thousand years, the shortest is the eighth part of a Palyōpamā. (220)

The longest duration of life in the Saudharmakalpa is two Sāgarōpamās, the shortest is one Palyōpamā. (221)

(In the same way (*a*) the longest, and (*b*) the shortest duration of life in the remaining Kalpas and heavenly regions is given in the original. I give in the sequel the substance only of each verse.)

In Īśāna Kalpa (*a*) is somewhat more than a Sāgarōpamā, (*b*) somewhat more than a Palyōpamā. (222)

In Sanatkumāra Kalpa (*a*) is seven, (*b*) two Sāgarōpamās. (223)

In Māhēndra Kalpa (*a*) is somewhat more than seven Sāgarōpamās, (*b*) somewhat more than two. (224)

In Brahmalōka Kalpa (*a*) is ten Sāgarōpamās, (*b*) seven. (225)

In Lantaka Kalpa (*a*) is fourteen Sāgarōpamās, (*b*) ten. (226)

In Mahāśukla Kalpa (*a*) is seventeen Sāgarōpamās, (*b*) fourteen.[77] (227)

In Sahasrāra Kalpa (*a*) is eighteen Sāgarōpamās, (*b*) seventeen. (228)

In ānata Kalpa (*a*) is nineteen Sāgarōpamās, (*b*) eighteen. (229)

In Prāṇata Kalpa (*a*) is twenty Sāgarōpamās, (*b*) nineteen. (230)

In āraṇa Kalpa (*a*) is twenty-one Sāgarōpamās, (*b*) twenty. (231)

In Achyuta Kalpa (*a*) is twenty-two Sāgarōpamās, (*b*) twenty-one. (232)

In the first (Graivēyika region) (*a*) is twenty-three Sāgarōpamās, (*b*) twenty-two. (233)

In the second (Graivēyika region) (*a*) is twenty-four Sāgarōpamās, (*b*) twenty-three. (234)

In the third (Graivēyika region) (*a*) is twenty-five Sāgarōpamās, (*b*) twenty-four. (235)

In the fourth (Graivēyika region) (*a*) is twenty-six Sāgarōpamās, (*b*) twenty-five. (236)

In the fifth (Graivēyika region) (*a*) is twenty-seven Sāgarōpamās, (*b*) twenty-six. (237)

In the sixth (Graivēyika region) (*a*) is twenty-eight Sāgarōpamās, (*b*) twenty-seven. (238)

In the seventh (Graivēyika region) (*a*) is twenty-nine Sāgarōpamās, (*b*) twenty-eight. (239)

In the eighth (Graivēyika region) (*a*) is thirty Sāgarōpamās, (*b*) twenty-nine. (240)

In the ninth (Graivēyika region) (*a*) is thirty-one Sāgarōpamās, (*b*) thirty. (241)

In the four heavens (of the Anuttara gods), beginning with Vijaya,[78] (*a*) is thirty-three Sāgarōpamās, (*b*) thirty-one. (242)

In the great Vimāna Sarvārtha(siddha) there is no difference between the longest and shortest duration of life, but it is always thirty-three Sāgarōpamās. (243)

The longest and shortest duration of the gods' (continuance in the same kind of) body is equal to that which has been given for their life. (244, 245[79], 246 = 159, 160)

We have described the Living Beings, the worldly and the perfected ones, and we have described the Lifeless Things, those possessing form and those without form. (247)

Having thus learned (the nature of) living beings and lifeless things which is in accordance with the principles of reasoning,[80] and believing in it, a sage should delight in self-control. (248)

After having lived as a Śramaṇa many years, a sage should mortify himself[81] by the following religious exercises. (249)

The longest duration of the mortification is twelve years; the middle, one year; and the shortest, six months. (250)

In the first four years he should abstain from dressed food,[82] in the second four years he should keep various fasts. (251)

During two years he should eat āchāmla[83] at the end of every second fast; in the following half year he should keep not too long fasts. (252)

In the second half of the year he should keep long fasts. During the whole year he should eat but small portions of Āchāmla. (253)

During the (last) year a sage should make the ends of two consecutive fasts meet,[84] and should break his fast after half a month or a whole month, (till he dies). (254)

The following (Bhāvanās), Kandarpa-, Abhiyōgika-, Kilviṣa-, Mōha-, and Asuratva-(Bhāvanās[85]), will lead to evil ways (*i.e.* bad births); they are obnoxious at the time of death. (255)

Those souls who cherish heretical opinions, commit sins, and kill living beings, will not reach Bōdhi at the time of death. (256)

Those souls who cherish orthodox opinions, do not commit sins, and are enveloped in white Lēśyā, will reach Bōdhi at the time of death. (257)

Those souls who cherish heretical opinions, commit sins, and are enveloped in black Lēśyā, will not reach Bōdhi at the time of death. (258)

Those who love the creed of the Jinas and piously practise it, will be pure and free from the soil (of passions), and will (in due time) get out of the Circle of Births. (259)

The miserable men who do not know the creed of the Jinas, will many times commit unholy suicide and die against their will. (260)

Those who are well versed in the sacred lore and possess much knowledge, who awaken piety (in others) and appreciate their good qualities, are for this very reason worthy to hear the doctrine of salvation.[86] (261)

He who by ribaldry and buffoonery, by his comical habits and appearance, by jests and words amuses other people, realises the Kandarpa-Bhāvanā. (262)

Those who practise spells and besmear their body with ashes for the sake of pleasure, amusement, or power, realise the Abhiyōgika-Bhāvanā.[87] (263)

The deceitful man who reviles the sacred lore, the Kēvalins, the teacher of the Law, the Saṅgha, and the monks, realises the Kilviṣika-Bhāvanā. (264)

He who is continuously angry, and who puts his faith in prognostics, realises the Asuratva-Bhāvanā. (265)

Those who use weapons, eat poison, throw themselves into fire or water, and use things not prescribed by the rules of good conduct, are liable to be born and to die again and again. (Such persons realise the Mōha-Bhāvanā.) (266)

The enlightened and liberated Jñātṛ(putra) has thus delivered

Thirty-six Lectures of the Uttarādhyayana,[88] which the pious[89] approve of. (267)

Here ends the Uttarādhyayana Sūtra

Notes

First Lecture

1. Āṇā-niddēsa-karē. Ājñā is the order itself; nirdēśa, the assent to it.

2. The original has the plural instead of the singular. It takes great liberties in this respect, and the commentators constantly call to help a vachanavyatyaya or liṅgavyatyaya, exchange of number or gender, as the case may be. It is impossible in the translation to follow the original in this respect, and useless to note all such grammatical blunders. The conclusion we may draw from them is that in the spoken language many grammatical forms which in the literary language continued to be used, were on the point of dying out or had already actually become obsolete. I am almost sure that the vernacular of the time when the Sūtras were composed began to drop the distinction between the singular and plural in the verb. It was, however, artificially revived in the literary Māhārāṣṭrī of later days.

3. Buddhaputta. Buddha is here and in the sequel explained by āchārya, teacher. The word is in the crude form, not in the inflected form, as the nominative would not suit the metre. Liberties of this kind are frequently met with in our text.

4. Niōgaṭṭhī = niyōgarthin. It is always explained and usually means mōkṣārthin. But here and in verse 20 niyōga has perhaps its common meaning: appointment, order. In that case we must translate: he who waits for an order.

5. Chaṇḍāliya, literally, he should not demean himself like a Chāṇḍāla. The commentators, however, divide the word in chanḍa, violent, hot, and alīka, untrue, false. This explanation is too artificial to be accepted, though the meaning comes to the same thing.

6. Buddhāṇaṃ, *i.e.* the superiors.

7. Palhatthiyā = paryastikā: so that his clothes cover his knees and shanks.

8. Pakṣapiṇḍa.

9. Niyāgaṭṭhī or niōgaṭṭhī. The commentator explains it, as in verse 7, by "desiring liberation."

10. Ukkuḍuō. The commentator explains it by muktāsanaḥ, kāraṇataḥ pādapuñchanādigataḥ.

11. In illustration of this the commentator (Dēvēndra) quotes the following verse: ēṣa bandhyāsutō yāti khapuṣpakṛtaśēkharaḥ | mṛgatṛṣṇāmbhasi snātaḥ śaśaśṛṅgadhanurdharaḥ || There goes the son of a barren woman, bearing a chaplet of sky-flowers, having bathed in the water of a fata morgana, and carrying a bow made of a hare's horn.

12. Samara, explained by the commentator barbers' shop or smithy, with the addition that it includes all places of low people.

13. Buddhāḥ.

14. Phāsuya, translated prāsuka, and explained: free from living beings.

15. Parakaḍa, prepared for the householder or some other person, but not for the monk himself.

16. The translation of the terms in this verse is rather conjectural, notwithstanding the explanations in the commentary.

17. I translate according to the interpretation of the commentator, which is probably right; but the text sets all rules of grammar at defiance.

18. Literally, search for the goad.

19. Buddha.

20. Namati, literally, bows down.

21. Puvvasaṃthuya = pūrvasaṃstuta. Besides the meaning rendered in my translation the commentator proposes another: already famous.

22. Aṭṭhiya = arthika, having an object or purpose, *viz.* mōkṣa; it is therefore frequently rendered: leading to liberation.

23. *i.e.* a liberated or perfected soul.

24. Ti bēmi = iti bravīmi. These words serve to mark the end of every chapter in all canonical books; compare the Latin dixi.

Second Lecture

1. Parīsaha, that which may cause trouble to an ascetic, and which must be cheerfully borne.

2. The commentator (Dēvēndra) says that when Mahāvīra spoke, he was understood by all creatures, whatever was their language. He quotes the following verse: dēvā dēvīṃ narā nārīṃ śabarāś chāpi śābarīṃ | tiryañcho pi cha tairaśchīṃ mēnirē bhagavadgiraṃ || The gods, men, Śabaras, and animals took the language of the Lord for their own. Cf. Acts ii. 11.

3. *i.e.* in our creed or religion. This is generally the meaning of the word iha, here, opening a sentence.

4. This is to include all biting or stinging insects, as lice, etc.

5. This is binding on the Jinakalpikas only, not on common monks.

6. The preceding part of this lecture is in prose, the rest is in ślōka. The numbers placed before the verses refer to the above enumeration of the troubles. It will be seen that two stanzas are allotted to each of them.

7. *i.e.* Mahāvīra, who belonged to the Gōtra of Kāśyapa.

8. Vigaḍa = vikṛta. It means water which by boiling or some other process has become so changed that it may be regarded as lifeless.

9. Lāḍha; see also Fifteenth Lecture, note 2.

10. *i.e.* in which there are no women.

11. Or like an ignorant man, bāla.

12. *viz.* if he falls sick.

13. Tantuja, what is manufactured from threads.

14. Nirjarā.

15. The commentators refer the word "anywhere" to the place or object of the former actions.

Third Lecture

1. About the Kunthu see below, Thirty-sixth Lecture, v. 138 and note.

2. One "former" (pūrva) year consists of 7,560 millions of common years. The idea that years were longer when the world was still young, is apparently suggested by the experience which everybody will have made, that a year seemed to us an enormously long time when we were young, and the same space of time appears to us shorter and shorter as we advance in life. A similar analogy with our life has probably caused the belief in the four ages of the world, shared by the Hindus and the ancients. For does not childhood to most of us appear the happiest period of our life, and youth better still than the time of full-grown manhood? As in retrospect our life appears to us, so primitive man imagines the life of the world to have been: the first age was the best and the longest, and the following ages grew worse and worse, and became shorter at the same time. This primitive conceit was by the ancients combined with the conceit of the year, so that the four ages were compared with the four seasons of the year. Something similar seems to have happened in India, where, however, there are three or six seasons. For the Jainas seem to have originally divided one Eon into six minor periods. Now the year was frequently compared to a wheel, and this second metaphor was worked out by the Jainas. They named the six minor periods aras, literally spokes of a wheel, and divided the whole Eon into one descending part (of the wheel), avasarpiṇī, and one rising part, utsarpiṇī. These Avasarpiṇīs and Utsarpiṇīs are probably a later improvement, and the Eon originally contained but six Aras. But if there were indeed twelve Aras from the beginning, they must have been suggested by the twelve months of the year.

3. This is the first of the ten kinds of men mentioned above; the remaining nine are enumerated in the following verse.

Fourth Lecture

1. A similar expression is used in Sūtrakṛtāṅga I, 2, 2, 21.

2. Dēvēndra relates two stories of burglars, one of which is supposed to be hinted at in the text. It comes to this. A burglar is caught, in the breach he had excavated, by the owner of the house, who takes hold of his feet protruding from the breach. But the burglar's companion tries to drag him out from the

other side of the wall. In this position he is smashed by the upper part of the wall coming down.

3. Each of these birds has two necks and three legs.

4. Upamā. Literally translated: "this is the comparison of those who contend that life is eternal." The commentator gives a forced interpretation of the first part of the verse to bring about a comparison. But the meaning "comparison" will not suit the context, the word must here mean: conclusion, reasoning.

Fifth Lecture

1. *viz.* in the case of a Kēvalin. Other sages die this death seven or eight times before reaching mukti.

2. Kālikā, doubtful as regards the time when they will be enjoyed.

3. *i.e.* I shall do as people generally do, *viz.* enjoy pleasures.

4. *viz.* By his acts and thoughts.

5. Saṃjayāṇaṃ vusīmao = saṃyatānāṃ vaśyavataṃ. Vusīmao is gen. sing., it is here used in juxtaposition with a word in gen. plur. Such an irregularity would of course be impossible in classical Prākṛt, but the authors of metrical Jaina Sūtras take such liberties with grammar that we must put up with any faulty expression, though it would be easy to correct it by a conjecture.

6. Kāēṇa phāsaē = kāyāna spṛśat, literally, touch with his body.

7. The Pōsaha of the Jainas corresponds to the Upōsatha of the Buddhists. Hoernle in note 87 of his translation of the Uvāsaga Dasāo [Upāsaka-daśāḥ] (Bibliotheca Indica) says of the Pōsaha: it is distinguished by the four abstinences (uvavāsa) from food (āhāra), bodily attentions (śarīrasatkāra), sexual intercourse (abrahma) and daily work (vyāpāra).

8. Literally, skin and joints.

9. These three methods are (1) bhaktapratyākhyāna, (2) iṅgitamaraṇa, (3) pādapōpagamana. They are fully described in the Āchārāṅga Sūtra I, 7, 8, 7 ff., see *Sacred Books of the East*, vol. 22, p. 75 f.

Sixth Lecture

1. Khuḍḍāganiyaṇṭhijjaṃ = Kṣullakanirgranthīyam. Kṣullaka originally means "small, young," but I do not see that the contents of this lecture support this translation, though the commentators would seem to favour it.

2. Dēvēndra here quotes the following Sanskrit verse: Kalatranigaḍaṃ dattvā na saṃtuṣṭaḥ prajāpatiḥ bhūyō-py apatyarūpēṇa dadāti galaśṛṅkhalam. The creator was not satisfied when he had given (to man) the wife as a fetter, he added a chain round his neck in the form of children.

3. This verse recurs in Sūtrakṛtāṅga I, 9, 5.

4. Sapēhāē pāsē = svaprēkṣayā paśyēt, he should look at it with his mind or reflectively. However sapēhāē is usually the absolute participle samprēkṣya. The meaning is the same in both cases.

5. Some MSS. insert here the following verse: "Movables and immovables, corn, and furniture can not deliver a man from pain, who is suffering for his deeds."

6. This is according to the commentators the meaning of the word dōguñchī = jugupsin.

7. Āyariyaṃ vidittāṇaṃ. The commentator makes this out to mean: by learning only what right conduct (āchārikam) is, without living up to it. But it is obvious that the author intends a censure upon the Jñānamārga.

8. As usual this phrase means: one should conduct one's self so as to commit no sin.

9. There is a pun in the original on the word patta, which means plumes (patra) and alms-bowl (pātra).

10. This is the ēṣaṇāsamiti. On the samitis see below, Twelfth Lecture, 2.

11. Vēsaliē = Vaiśālīka. See my remarks on this statement in *Sacred Books of the East*, vol. 22, introduction, p. xi, and Hoernle's notes in his translation of the Uvāsaga Dasāo, p. 3 ff.

Seventh Lecture

1. Yavasa, explained by mudgamāṣādi. Mutton of gram-fed sheep is greatly appreciated in India.

2. Aya = aja, literally goat.

3. Chuya = kyuta is said of one who is born after his death in a lower sphere than that in which he lived before.

4. According to the commentators the eightieth part of a rupee.

5. The commentators relate "old stories" to explain allusions in the text; they will, however, be intelligible without further comment, though I do not contend that those stories were not really old and known to the author of the Sūtra.

6. A nayuta or niyuta is equal to

49,786,136,000,000,000,000,000,000,000,000.

It is derived in the following way:

1 pūrvāṅga = 8,400,000

1 pūrva = 8,400,000 pūrvāṅgas.

1 nayutāṅga = 8,400,000 pūrvas.

1 nayuta = 8,400,000 nayutāṅgas.

7. This parable closely corresponds to Matth. xxv. 14, Luke xix. 11. I need not here discuss the problems raised by this coincidence since they will, as I hear,

be fully treated by Herr Hüttemann, a pupil of Professor Leumann of Strassburg.

8. Lōlayāsaḍhē = lōlatāśaṭha. The commentator takes lōlatā for lōla and makes the word a karmadhāraya. I think that the word śaṭha which originally means "one who deceives others" is used here in the sense "one who deceives himself."

9. *i.e.* birth as a man or a god.

10. Śikṣā. The commentator quotes the following passage in Prākṛt: Souls gain human birth through four causes: (1) a kind disposition (prakṛtibhadratā), (2) love of discipline (prakṛtivinītatā), (3) compassion (sānukrośanatā), and (4) want of envy (amatsaritā).

11. For a higher rank than that of a god, *e.g.* that of a Kēvalin, cannot, in the present state of the world, be attained.

Eighth Lecture

1. This lecture is ascribed to Kapila. According to an old story, told in the commentary, he was the son of Kāśyapa, a Brahman of Kauśāmbī, and his wife Yaśā. When Kāśyapa died, his place was given to another man. His wife then sent her boy to Śrāvastī to study under Indradatta, a friend of his father's. That man was willing to instruct the boy, and procured him board and lodging in a rich merchant's house. Kapila, however, soon fell in love with the servant-girl who was appointed to his service. Once, at a festival kept by her caste, the girl in tears told him that she could not take part in the festivity as she had no money to buy ornaments. To get some she asked him to go to Dhana, a merchant, who used to give two pieces of gold to the man who saluted him first in the morning. Accordingly Kapila set out in the night, but was taken up by the police and brought before the king, Praśēnajit. The student made a clear breast before the king, who was so pleased with him that he promised to give him whatever he should ask. Kapila went in the garden to consider what he should ask; and the more he thought about it, the more he raised the sum which he believed he wanted, till it came to be ten thousand millions. But then, all of a sudden, the light came upon him; he began to repent of the sinful life he had led up to that time, and tearing out his hair he became a Svayaṃsaṃbuddha. Returning to the king, he pronounced verse 17: The more you get, etc., and giving him the Dharmalābha, he went his way. He practised austerities and acquired superior knowledge, by dint of which he came to know that in a wood, eighteen leagues from Rājagṛha, lived a gang of five hundred robbers, under a chief Balabhadra. These men, he knew, would become converts to the right faith; accordingly he went to the wood where they lived. He was made prisoner, and brought before the leader of the robbers. To have some fun out of him they ordered him to dance, and on his objecting

that there was none to play up, they all clapped their hands to beat the time. He then sang the first stanza of this lecture, by which some robbers were converted, and he continued to sing, repeating this stanza after each following verse (as dhruva), till at last all the robbers were converted.

2. The commentator quotes the following words: brahmaṇē brāhmaṇam ālabhēta, indrāya kṣattram, marudbhyō vaiśyaṃ, tapasē śūdram, and explains them: he who kills a Brāhmaṇa will acquire Brahma knowledge.

3. See the note on verse 17 of the Fifteenth Lecture.

4. Samādhiyōgāḥ. Samādhi is concentration of the mind, and the yōgās are, in this connection, the operations (vyāpāra) of mind, speech, and body conducive to it.

5. Rākṣasīs in the original.

Ninth Lecture

1. The Life of king Nami and his Bōdhi is told in the commentary. The Prākṛt text of this romance is printed in my "Ausgewählte Erzählungen in Māhārāṣṭrī," Leipzig, 1886, p. 41 ff. Nami is one of the four simultaneous Pratyēkabuddhas, *i.e.* one of those saints who reach the highest stage of knowledge by an effort of their own, not through regular instruction and religious discipline. The Pratyēkabuddhas or Svayaṃsaṃbuddhas (Sahasambuddha in Prākṛt) do not, however, propagate the true Law, as the Tīrthakaras do. As the legend of Nami is not materially connected with our text, I need not give an abstract of it here.

2. The text has Mahilāē, which is against the metre. The locative makes the construction needlessly involved.

3. Chēiē, chaitya. The commentator interprets it as meaning udyāna, park; but to make good his interpretation he takes vacchē for an instrumental plural instead of a nominative singular. The context itself seems to militate against this interpretation; for it is natural to say of a tree that it has many leaves, but it is rather strained to say the same of a park.

4. An instrument for defending a town.

5. Gacchasi. The commentator explains this as an imperative, but there is no necessity for it.

6. Tigutta, this is a pun on the three guptis.

7. Vardhamānagṛha; the houses which are so called, belong to the best kind, see Varāha Mihira, Bṛhat Saṃhitā 53, 36.

8. The first line of this verse is in the Āryā-metre, the second in Anuṣṭubh; the whole will not construe, but the meaning is clear. There are numerous instances in which the metre changes in the same stanza from āryā to Anuṣṭubh, and vice versa, so frequent they are that we are forced to admit the

fact that the authors of these metrical texts did not shrink from taking such liberties.

9. Ghōrāsama. A Jaina author cannot forbear to name things from his religious point of looking at them. Thus only can it be explained that here Indra is made to apply to the āśrama of the householder an attribute which not he but his opponent could have used. Our verse is, however, probably only a later addition, as it has not the burden of the verses put into the mouth of Indra.

10. The wheel and the hook.

Tenth Lecture

1. This is a sermon delivered by Mahāvīra to his disciple Indrabhūti, who belonged to the Gōtama Gōtra. In the commentary a lengthy legend is given how Gautama came to want this instruction. As it is not necessary for understanding the contents of this lecture, I may pass it over.

2. Verses 5-9 treat of the ēkēndriyas or beings which possess but one organ of sense, that of touch. A full description of them as well as of the dvīndriyas, etc. is given in the last lecture.

3. The periods called asaṃkhya are measured by utsarpiṇīs and avasarpiṇīs which correspond to the kalpas of the Hindus, but greatly exaggerated. An asaṃkhya is the longest time (ukkōsaṃ = utkarṣaṃ) which a soul may be doomed to live in earth-bodies; see Thirty-Sixth Lecture, 81 ff.

4. This is, according to the commentary, the meaning of duranta.

5. A saṃkhijja, *i.e.* saṃkhyēya, is a period which can be measured by thousands of years.

6. This attribute is here given to "water," because in autumn the water becomes pure, and even the purest water has no hold upon the leaves of a lotus; thus a saint should give up even the best and dearest attachment.

7. As this assertion cannot be put in the mouth of Mahāvīra, this verse must be set down as a later addition—or perhaps as a blunder of the poet similar to that noted before, in the Ninth Lecture, 42 (note 8).

8. This seems, according to the commentary, to be the meaning of the phrase akalēvarasēṇim ūsiyā. Akalēvaraśrēṇī is said to mean as much as kṣapakaśrēṇī.

9. Buddha.

10. Būhaē = vṛṃhayēt; literally, propagate.

11. Here the word buddha is used as a title; but its use is very restricted, scarcely going beyond that of a common epithet. This is just what we otherwise should have to assume in order to explain the use by the Bauddhas of that word to denote the founder of their sect. In the Sūtrakṛtāṅga II, 6, 28

Buddha, in the plural, actually denotes the prophets of the Buddhists.

Eleventh Lecture

1. Literally, who always remains in his teacher's kula.

2. Kanthaka. The horse of Buddha is called Kanthaka; our passage shows that the word is not a proper noun, but an appellative.

3. This is the burden of all verses down to verse 30.

4. I have supplied these words here and in the following verses. The commentators try to do without them, and labour to point out qualities of the monk, which correspond to the attributes of the subject of the comparison.

5. Eugenia Jambu. According to the commentators the very tree is meant from which Jambūdvīpa took its name. They make of the presiding (āṇāḍhiya) deity, the god Anādṛta. I am not prepared to say that there is such a god as Anādṛta. The name looks suspicious. I think āṇāḍhiya is equal to ājñāsthita.

6. According to the cosmography of the Jainas the Śītā is a river which takes its rise in the Nīla range and falls into the Eastern ocean. The Nīla is the fourth of the six parallel mountain-barriers, the southernmost of which is the Himālaya. (Trailōkya Dīpikā, Umāsvātis' Tattvārthādhigama Sūtra, etc.)

7. This epithet apparently refers to Viṣṇu's sleeping on the ocean.

Twelfth Lecture

1. The commentators relate a legend of the principal figure in the following lecture. We may skip his former births and begin with his last. Near the Ganges lived Balakōṣṭha, chief of a Chāṇḍāla tribe, called Harikēśa (the yellow-haired). With his wife Gaurī he had a son Bala, who in the course of time became a Jaina monk and a great Ṛṣi. On his wanderings he once stayed in the Tinduga-grove near Benares, the presiding deity of which, a Yakṣa, became his most fervent follower. One day Bhadrā, king Kausalika's daughter, came to the Yakṣa's shrine and paid homage to the idol. But seeing the dirty monk, she did not conceal her aversion. The Yakṣa, however, to punish her for her want of respect for the holy man, possessed her. As no physician or conjurer could cure her madness, the Yakṣa, by whom she was possessed, said she would recover only if she were offered as bride to Bala, the monk. The king agreeing, Bhadrā became sound as before and went to the monk to choose him for her husband. Bala of course refused her. She was then married by the king to his Purōhita, Rudradēva, whose sacrifice-enclosure is the scene of the occurrences related in the Twelfth Lecture.

2. These are the five Samitis. Compare Bhandarkar, Report on the Search for Sanskrit Manuscripts for 1883-84, p. 98, note †.

3. These are the three Guptis. Compare Bhandarkar, loc. cit. p. 100, note *.

4. Piśācha. A full description of a Piśācha is given in the Uvāsaga Dasāo, § 94 of Hoernle's edition.

5. This reminds one of the biblical parable of the sower.

6. The word Nirgrantha has here, besides its common meaning, Jaina monk, another derived from its etymological meaning, "without any tie, without restraint," *i.e.* shameless.

7. For Samiti and Gupti see notes 2 and 3.

8. Saṃvara is preventing, by means of the Samitis and Guptis, the āsrava, or flowing in of the Karman upon the soul. Bhandarkar, loc. cit. p. 106.

9. This is the Kāyōtsarga, the posture of a man standing with all his limbs immovable, by which he fortifies himself against sins, etc.

10. Attapasannalēsa = ātmaprasannalēśya, "in which the Lēśyā is favourable for the soul." The Lēśyā is comparable to the subtile body of the orthodox philosophy. The theory of the Lēśyā forms the subject of the Thirty-fourth Lecture.

11. Dōsa, which means hatred (dvēṣa) and impurity (dōṣa).

Thirteenth Lecture

1. The stories about Chitra and Sambhūta and the fate they underwent in many births are common to Brahmans, Jainas, and Buddhists. The whole subject has been exhaustively dealt with by Prof. Leumann in two learned papers in the Winer Zeitschrift für die Kunde des Morgenlandes, vol. V, pp. I ff., III ff., where an analysis of the various documents which relate this legend is given, and the Prākṛt text of the Thirteenth and Fourteenth Lectures together with a German translation is published. For all details, therefore, the reader is referred to Prof. Leumann's papers.

2. The commentator constructs Chitra with dhaṇappabhūya: full of manifold treasures; but Prof. Leumann is probably right in taking it as a vocative.

3. Ādāna, explained charitradharma.

4. This might be translated, as Professor Leumann suggests: possessing Karman as the germ (of his future destiny); still I prefer the meaning vouched for by the commentators, because karmabīja generally means the germ, *i.e.* cause of Karman, see below, Thirty-second Lecture, verse 7.

5. See Professor Leumann's remarks on this verse, l.c., p. 137 f.

6. When Sunandā, wife of Sanatkumāra, paid homage to Sambhūta, then a Jaina monk, and touched his feet with the curls of her soft hair, he was possessed by the desire to become a universal monarch in reward for his penances. This is the nidāna of which the text speaks, and what I render in this connection by "taking a resolution." For the story itself, see my Ausgewählte

Erzählungen in Māhārāṣṭrī, p. 5 f.

Fourteenth Lecture

1. In Prākṛt Usuyāra (or Isuyāra). According to the Prākṛt legend given in the commentary it was in the Kuru country.

2. Sattā in the original; it is rendered sattva by the commentators. Perhaps sattā is the Prākṛt for svātmā; at any rate, the context of the next verse proves that soul is intended.

3. Amūrta. In later philosophy mūrtatva is defined as the possessing of definite and limited form (paricchinnaparimāṇavattvam) or the possessing of action (kriyāvattvam or vegavattvam). Amūrta dravya are with the Vaiśeṣikas: the air (ākāśa), time, space, and Atman. These are also called nityadravya. Amūrta is here apparently synonymous with arūpin, formless, compare Lecture Thirty-Six, 4, where dharma, adharma, akāśa, and kāla are enumerated as the "formless things without life."

4. Literally, the nights. It seems to have been the custom at the time when the Sūtras were composed, to reckon the time by nights, though the reckoning by days is not quite uninstanced in the Sūtras.

5. This is the explanation of duhaō by the commentators, who apparently think that the parents and the sons are meant. The word in question is originally an adverb, but it is also (cf. Thirteenth Lecture, verse 18) taken by the commentator as a numeral, and rendered dvayōḥ. A genitive of the dual occurs in Lecture 19, 90.

6. Cyprinus Rohita.

7. It was considered a privilege of the king to confiscate the property of a man who had no heir; compare Gautama, Lecture Twenty-Eight, 42, Vasiṣṭha, Lecture 17, 83-86, etc.

8. This apparently refers to the birds mentioned in the last verse.

9. Kulala in the original. Kulāla in Sanskrit denotes the wild cock, Phasianus Gallus. The word seems to be derived from kulāya by assimilation of the y to the preceding consonant, compare saliyā for sallyā = saritā = sarit. In the sense of bird the word kulāla seems to be used in the well-known stanza of A Bhartṛhari: brahmā yena kulālavan niyamito brahmāṇḍabhāṇḍōdare, unless here kulāla is an early corruption for kulāyin.

10. The commentators assign these verses to the two sons of Bhṛgu; but then the verses do not construe. Besides the mention of the "large kingdom" in the first line seems to prove that the king, and not the Brahmans, is to be understood as the person addressed. In the last line I separate pagijjhaha kkhāyaṃ (scil. tavaṃ), instead of pagijjh-ahakkhāyaṃ. It is, however, just possible that the next verse is to be connected with the preceding ones; in that

case, we must read pagijjh- and interpret it in conformity with the scholiast as a gerund.

11. The bhāvanās are certain meditations which are conducive to the purity of the soul. They are treated at length in a work by Hēmachandra, called Bhavabhāvanā, which seems to be rather popular with the Śvētāmbaras. The Digambaras seem to call them Anuprēkṣās. A work in Prākṛt by Śubhachandra, called Kārttikēyānuprēkṣā, is epitomised in Bhandarkar's Report for 1883-84, p. 113 ff.

Fifteenth Lecture

1. The name of this lecture, sa bhikkhū, is derived from the burden which runs through the whole of it and winds up every verse.

2. Lāḍhē, explained sadaṇuṣṭhānatayā pradhānaḥ. Lāḍha is also the name of a country in western Bengal, inhabited, at Mahāvīra's time, by uncivilised tribes, see *Sacred Books of the East*, vol. 22, p. 84, note 1. The etymology of both words is doubtful.

3. Compare the note on p. 161 of *Sacred Books of the East*, vol. 22. The 71st chapter of Varāha Mihira's Bṛhat Saṃhitā treats of vastrachēda, rents, etc. of clothes; the 51st, of aṅgavidyā, forebodings from the body; and the 53rd, of vāstuvidyā, property of buildings; chapters 88, 90, and 95 are devoted to the forebodings from the cries of birds, female jackals, and crows.

4. A conjectural rendering of vijaya, which cannot be taken in its ordinary meaning "victory." The commentary explains it śubhāśubhanirūpaṇābhyāsaḥ. —Notice the absence of astrology from the above list of prophetical arts practised by strolling friars apparently to insinuate themselves into the good graces of laymen and women. If Greek nativity had already risen to importance, it certainly would have been mentioned. For it has ever since held a firm hold on the Hindu mind.—This remark also applies to Lecture Twenty 45. But in Sūtrakṛtāṅga I, 12, 9, astrology (saṃvacchara) is mentioned; it is, however, the ancient astrology of the Hindus, not the Greek one.

5. The Ugras and Bhōgas were Kṣatriyas. The former were, according to the Jainas, descendants of those whom Ṛṣabha, the first Tīrthakara, appointed to the office of kōṭwals or prefects of towns, while the Bhōgas were descendants from those whom Ṛṣabha acknowledged as persons deserving of honour. Comp. Hoernle, Uvāsaga Dasāo, Appendix, p. 58, and my edition of the Kalpa Sūtra, p. 103, note on § 18.

6. The commentators supply these words; something to that purport is wanted to make out a consistent meaning, but there is not so much as a hint of it in the text itself. As it stands now, the meaning would be just the opposite of that given in the translation, which is in better accordance with the established custom.

7. Āyāmaga, it is rendered āchāmaka in Sanskrit, and explained avaśrāvaṇa, *i.e.* avasrāvaṇa. See also Leumann, Aupapātika Sūtra, Glossary sv.

8. Sauvīra, explained kāñjika, the water of boiled rice in a state of spontaneous fermentation.

9. This is a later addition, proved to be such by the metre, though the commentators comment upon it.

10. Khēyāṇugaē. The commentators explain khēda by saṃyama.

Sixteenth Lecture

1. The word "here" is explained as meaning "in this religion of the Jainas." See Second Lecture, note 3.

2. Saṃvara is the stopping of the āsravas by means of the Samitis and Guptis, see Twelfth Lecture, note 9.

3. Literally, beds and seats.

4. This might also be rendered: he should not talk about women.

5. The preceding part of this lecture is in prose.

6. Iṭṭhaṃ cha, *i.e.* iṣṭaṃ cha. The commentators connect the words with the second part of the sentence. By giving to cha the meaning of api they interpret the two words in question as meaning "though very pleasant."

7. Tālauḍa. According to the Dīpikā it is a poison which kills by merely touching the palate (tālukasparśanamātrād ēva); but this is a mere guess prompted by a wrong etymology. Tālauḍa stands perhaps for tālakūṭa, which may have been a variant of kālakūṭa, the deadly poison swallowed by Śiva.

8. Here we have twice the same word dhammārāmē, which I haveonce translated "park of the Law," and then "vessel of righteousness." It is obvious that a play on this word is intended, though I may have failed to hit the meaning of the author.

Seventeenth Lecture

1. Pādakambala, usually called rajōharaṇa. One commentator suggests, as a possible rendering, pātrakambala "a cloth to cover his almsbowl."

2. It is a monk's duty closely to inspect everything that he uses or comes in contact with, in order to avoid hurting inadvertently anything considered to possess life. This is called paḍilēhā.

3. Gāṇaṃgaṇika, according to the commentators one who attaches himself to another gaṇa every half-year.

4. Sāmudāṇiya, explained bhaiksham.

5. Pañchakuśīla, literally, those who practise the five wrong śīlas, whereby probably those are denoted who do not keep the five great vows of the Jainas. Note that the Buddhists too have their pañchaśīla. They could therefore have

been called pañchakuśīla by the Jainas.

6. The text is not settled in the last line; but there can be no doubt about the meaning.

Eighteenth Lecture

1. The commentators Sankritise this name in Saṃyata. But however appropriate it may be to a Jaina, it certainly does not look like a king's name. The Sanskrit form of the name was probably Sañjaya or Sṛñjaya, both of which frequently occur in Sanskrit literature.

2. To render āsrava.

3. Apphōva in the original; there are several plants which are called āsphōta.

4. Literally, a Brahman

5. Buddhē, explained āchāryān, preceptors.

6. These are the four great heresies: (1) that of the kriyāvādinas, who maintain that the soul exists; (2) that of the akriyāvādinas, who hold the reverse of the preceding doctrine; (3) that of the vainayikas, which seems to be identical with salvation by bhakti; (4) that of the ajñānavādinas, who contend that knowledge is not necessary for salvation, but t a p a s; this seems identical with the karmapatha. The commentators explain kriyāvādinaḥ "those who believe the soul or ātman to be characterised by the verb to be (*i.e.* by a permanent and unchangeable existence), and ascribe to it such qualities as ubiquity or non-ubiquity, activity or non-activity." This they treat as heresy, but from Mahāvagga VI, 31, 2 (vol. xvii, p. 109) it is evident that the Jainas were considered kriyāvādins. The akriyāvāda is also identified with the kṣaṇikavāda or doctrine, usually ascribed to Buddhists, that everything has but a momentary existence and is in the next moment replaced by a facsimile of itself. About these heresies compare the Sūtrakṛtāṅga I, 12; II, 2, 77.

7. According to the commentary a pālī seems to be what is commonly called palyōpamā, and mahāpālī a sāgarōpamā. However the longest life of a god in Brahmalōka is but ten Sāgarōpamās, see Lecture Thirty-Six, 225. The construction of the verse is very involved, but the drift of it cannot be mistaken.

8. ii vijjām aṇusaṃcharē. I believe that vijjām here stands for vidvān, as in the following verse. The meaning would then be, "knowing this one should live as a monk."

9. Buddha.

10. The Jainas do not deny the existence of the soul, but the unalterable character of the soul. Hence they object to the kriyāvāda.

11. Bharata was the eldest son of Riṣabha, the first Tīrthakara. He became the first Chakravartin, or universal monarch, and resided in Ayōdhyā. At his

renunciation he was ordered by Indra himself to pluck out five handfuls of his hair as is the custom of Jaina monks on entering the order.

12. Sagara, king of Ayōdhyā, was, according to the legend contained in the commentary (see R. Fick, Eine jainistische Bearbeitung der Sagara-Sage, Kiel, 1889), the younger brother of Ajita, the second Tīrthakara. He became the second Chakravartin, and, in the end, he was ordained by Ajita. The Jaina legend seems to be but a strangely distorted version of the story of Sagara told in the first book of the Rāmāyaṇa.

13. Maghavan, son of king Samudravijaya of Śrāvastī, and his wife Bhadrā, became the third Chakravartin.

14. Sanatkumāra, son of king Aśvasēna of Hastināpura, and his wife Sahadēvī, became the fourth Chakravartin. The adventures of Sanatkumāra are told in a Prākṛt legend, which I have published in my Ausgewählte Erzählungen in Māhārāṣṭrī, Leipzig, x886, p. 20 ff.

15. Sànti was the sixteenth Tīrthakara, Kunthu the senventeenth, and Ara the eighteenth Tīrthakara. Kunthu sounds strange for a proper name. I think it just possible that it is a popular or Prākṛt corruption of Kakutsthu, who was an Aikṣvāka. As is well known, Rāma is frequently called after him Kākutstha, and so are other kings of the same line, in which he stands as the twenty-fifth according to the list in the Rāmāyaṇa I, 70.

16. Mahāpadma was the ninth Chakravartin. His elder brother was Viṣṇukumāra, who was ordained by Suvrata, a disciple of Munisuvrata, the twentieth Tīrthakara. He wrenched the sovereignty of the world from Namuchi, minister of his father Padmōttara, who had ascended the throne, by making him promise as much of his territory as he could cover with three strides. This is the Brahmanical story of Viṣṇu and Bali, for whom the Jainas have substituted Namuchi. According to them the minister Namuchi was, in a disputation, defeated by the Jaina monks, and to revenge himself on them, he ordered them to quit his kingdom as soon as he got it.—Mahāpadma's residence was Hastināpura.

17. Hariṣēṇa, son of king Mahāhari of Kāmpilya, became the tenth Chakravartin.

18. Jaya, son of king Samudravijaya of Rājagṛha, became the eleventh Chakravartin.

19. King Daśārṇabhadra was a contemporary of Mahāvīra.

20. These are the four Pratyēkabuddhas; see the Ninth Lecture, note 1.

21. The story of Udāyaṇa (or perhaps Uddāyana) will be found in my Ausgewählte Erzählungen in Māhārāṣṭrī, p. 28 ff. He was contemporary with Mahāvīra.

22. He was Nandana, the seventh Baladēva, son of king Agniśikha of Benares.

23. He was the son of king Brahmarāja of Dvārakāvatī, and eldest brother of the Vāsudēva Dviprṣṭa or Dvipuṣṭi.

24. To render aṇaṭṭhakati, of which the commentators offer several explanations, rendering it anārttākīrti and anaṣṭakīrti. A various reading āṇaṭṭhākitti is mentioned, and explained ājñā-artha-ākṛti.

25. Mahābala was the son of king Bala of Hastināpura. He lived at the time of Vimala, the thirteenth Tīrthakara.

Nineteenth Lecture

1. According to the commentators the Dōgundaka gods are the trāyastriṃśa gods. The Sanskrit of dōgundaga would be dvikundaka.

2. I separate the words pāsāy-ālōyaṇaṭṭhiō. The commentators take them for a compound; but then the preceding part of the sentence would not construe. It is an irregular sandhi, instances of which, however, are not unfrequent.

3. Cucumis Colocynthus.

4. *i.e.* food, drink, dainties, and spices.

5. Literally, well washed or bathed.

6. This appears to be the meaning of the words ahīv'ēgantadiṭṭhīē. We might perhaps take ahīv for ahivaṃ = ahivat, in which case the construction of the sentence would be grammatically correct. An alternative rendering would be: "(A monk) like a snake must have his eyes always open on the difficult conduct, O son." It is a well-known fact that snakes cannot shut their eyes as other animals.

7. Kotthala, a Dēśī-word for kuśūla, granary, see Hēmachandra, Dēśī Kōṣa 2, 48. The commentators render it by "cloth."

8. *viz.* those of the five senses.

9. The description of hell is a favourite theme with the monks of all ages and all religions; and the Jaina monks are not behind others in the treatment of this gruesome subject. A detailed description of the different hells will be found in the fifth lecture of the first book of the Sūtrakṛtāṅga. I remember a yati showing me, with much complacency, a manuscript of the latter work adorned with lively illustrations of the most exquisite tortures.

10. These are two rivers in hell; the sand of the one consists of vajra (either steel-filings or diamonds), and that of the other, of turmeric.

11. Karavattakarakayāīhiṃ = karapattrakrakachādibhiḥ.

12. Kōlasuṇaya, explained by śūkaraśvan, hog-dog, which may be a kind of hog or dog, probably the latter.

13. Samilā jue. The commentators render jue by yuga and yuta, and do not explain samilā, which they treat as a Sanskrit word. I think it is the Prākṛt of

samidh, compare vijjulā = vidyut, salilā = sarit.

14. Rojjho = ṛśya, see Hēmachandra, Dēśī Kōṣa 7, 12.

15. Ḍhaṅka gṛdhra. The commentators offer no explanation of ḍhaṅka, but only say that they are not real vultures as there are no animals in hell. Therefore they must be vaikriya, *i.e.*, in our case, demons who have adopted the shape of vultures.

16. The water of the river Vaitaraṇī consists of a very caustic acid.

17. Here and in the following verses the suffering of Mṛgāputra as an animal and a plant seems to be described. But in verse 68 the scene is again laid in hell. The first word in verse 63, etc., "as," would literally be "like" (viva in the original text), but in rendering it by "like," we have to assume that as a denizen of hell he is treated in the manner described, which seems rather strained.

18. Kuhāḍā = kuṭhāra; comp. pihaḍa = piṭhara. The form kuhārā occurs in Guzeratī, Sindhī, and Panjābī.

19. Kumāra; this is obviously the modern kamār "blacksmith" (derived from karmakāra); and it is of interest to find this form in an old text like the Uttarādhyayana.

20. To render surā, sīdhu, mairēya, and madhu.

21. Miga = mṛga, literally "antelope"; but here as frequently the word has apparently the more general meaning "wild animal."

22. See Twelfth Lecture, notes 2 and 3.

23. Gārava = gaurava or garva. Dīpikā: ṛddhigārava-rasagārava-sātāgārava iti garvatrayarahitaḥ.

24. To render daṇḍasallabhaēsu.

25. Vāsīchandaṇakappō. The author of the Avachūri explains this phrase thus: he did not like more a man who anoints himself with sandal than a mason. Apparently he gives to vāsa the meaning "dwelling"; but I think that the juxtaposition of chandana calls for a word denoting a bad-smelling substance, perhaps "ordure."

26. Literally "door." The meaning of the line will be fully rendered and the simile at least partially be preserved by the following less literal translation: he shut the door, as it were, to evil influences. For the āsrava, see Sixteenth Lecture, note 2.

Twentieth Lecture

1. Atthadhammagaiṃ = arthadharmagati. I think this equal to artha dharma mōkṣa, though the commentators offer a different explanation by making gati mean jñāna. The phrase is derived from the typical expression kāmārthadharmamōkṣa by leaving out kāma, which of course could not be

admitted by ascetics.

2. He is identical with Bimbisāra of the Buddhists; see my edition of the Kalpa Sūtra, introduction, p. 2.

3. The following verses prove that chaitya denotes park here as the word is explained by the scholiast in Lecture Nine, 9.

4. Nandana is Indra's park.

5. Bhadantāṇaṃ.

6. The verb is wanting in this verse, and there is an apparent tautology in the words as they now stand. This is an obvious mark of a corruption in the text, which, however, I do not know how to remove by a plausible conjecture.

7. Potthaṃ or pocchaṃ. The commentators are at a loss to give an etymology of this word, or rather have a choice of them to offer, which comes to the same thing, and proves that nothing certain was known. If potthā is the correct form, it may be derived from pra + ut + sthā, and mean "origin"; if pocchā or pucchā is the right spelling it is pṛcchā, and may mean "etymology."

8. Purāṇa purabhēdaṇī. As usual the commentators give a purely etymological explanation. But it is obvious that purabhēdana must have a similar meaning as purandara = Indra, or purabhid Śiva. The latter word occurs in later literature only, and, besides, Siva does not yet seem to have been generally acknowledged as the supreme god, when and where the Jaina Sūtras were composed. The Vedic word pūrbhid, "destroyer of castles," also presents itself as an analogy; though it is not yet the exclusive epithet of a god, it is frequently applied to Indra.

9. To render antariccha or antarittha. The Guzeratī translation renders it hṛdaya.

10. Chāuppāya = Chatuḥpāda. Four branches of medical science are intended.

11. Phiṭṭai = bhraśyati, Hēmachandra's Prākṛt Grammar, iv, 177.

12. See Nineteenth Lecture, Verse 52 etc.

13. The verses 38-53 are apparently a later addition because (1) the subject treated in them is not connected with that of the foregoing part, and (2) they are composed in a different metre.

14. These are the five Samitis, see Twelfth Lecture, Verse 2 etc.

15. Pollā or pullā, explained antaḥ-suṣira "hollow in the middle."

16. Ayantita = ayantrita. My translation is but conjectural. Perhaps the regular coins are not meant, but stamped lumps of metal, which were current long before coins were introduced.

17. Literally, "the flag of the seers"; the broom etc. are meant.

18. Kuhēḍavigjā.

19. Nirāsava = nirāsrava. For the āsravas, see Sixteenth Lecture, note 2.

Twenty-First Lecture

1. To render nītikōvida.

2. For Dōgundaga, see Nineteenth Lecture, note 1.

3. Saggantha = sagrantha, which is obviously the opposite of nirgrantha. The commentators correct saṃgaṃtha in saṃgaṃ cha. The original reading is in MS. B. A. has saṃgaṃtha, and so had C. originally, but it corrects the tha into cha. According to the commentators we should translate: abandoning worldly attachment which causes great distress, great delusion, black (Lēśyā), and dangers, one should, etc.

4. Paryāya-dharma. Paryāya means a state under which a substance presents itself. Here is meant the state of the soul in pravrajyā, *i.e.* śrāmaṇya-paryāya; compare the expressions chadmastha-paryāya and kēvali-paryāya. Paryāya-dharma is here equal to prayrajyā-dharma, Law of the monks.

5. Kālēṇa kālaṃ, the commentators supply kurvan, and explain the passage as follows: kālēna, *i.e.* in a pauruṣī (four hours) less one quarter of it, kālam, *i.e.* what is proper for the time. The meaning would be "doing at every time what is proper or prescribed to do at it." But this explanation looks very artificial; I think that the expression kalēṇa kālaṃ is an adverb of the same type as majjhaṃ majjhēṇa and many others.

6. Saṃjae. This word may be saṃyata in this place; but in verse 20, where the same line occurs again, it cannot be so interpreted, because there the word saṃjae occurs twice; once it has the meaning of saṃjata, but in the passage under discussion it must be a verb, and it is rendered there sañjayet = saṅgaṃ kuryāt by the commentators.

7. Akukkuō, translated akukūja, derived from the root kūj "to warble, to groan"; it would therefore mean "without complaint." But in I, 30 we have appakukkuē, derived from the root kuch "to bend, to be crooked," and it is rendered alpaspandana. The same meaning applies in the present case.

8. This is the meaning commonly given to the frequently occurring phrase arairaisahe. Another interpretation is: saṃyamā-saṃyamaviṣayē, tābhyāṃ na bādhatē.

9. Nirōvalēvāi = nirupalipta. By upalēpa may be meant "dirt," but the author of the Avachūri explains upalēpa as consisting in abhiṣvaṅga affection: It is almost impossible to render satisfactorily so vague an expression.

10. Niranganа = saṃyamē niśchala, immovable with regard to self-control.

Twenty-Second Lecture

1. According to the Brahmanical account Vasudēva lived in Mathurā. The name given to the town by the Jainas is apparently derived from Śauri, an epithet of Kṛṣṇa, whose grandfather was Śūra. Soriyapura may be Śaurikapura

or Śauryapura. The latter rendering adopted by our commentators is based on a wrong etymology.

2. Rāīmai, Rāimaī, and Rāyamatī are the forms of her name in Prākṛt; the spellings Rājimatī and Rājamatī are also met with in Sanskrit.

3. *viz.* Ugrasēna. He was placed on the throne by Kṛṣṇa on the death of Kaṃsa, cf. Viṣṇu Purāṇa V, 21. He and Dēvaka were the sons of āhuka, Kaṃsa was a son of Ugrasēna, and Dēvakī a daughter of Dēvaka, loc. cit. IV, 14. According to the legend of Kṛṣṇa, as told by the Brahmans and Jainas, Jarāsandha afterwards repeatedly attacked Mathurā. Kṛṣṇa therefore built Dvārakā on the shore of the western ocean, and sent thither the Yādava tribe, loc. cit. V, 22 and 23. The events narrated in the text must be understood to have occurred in Dvārakā, as is evident from verse 21.

4. Gandhahastin, an elephant of the best class, whose very smell is sufficient, as is believed, to frighten common elephants, see verse 55.

5. Dasāra in Prākṛt. They are a clan descended from Yadu.

6. In verse 10 Ariṣṭanēmi rides on an elephant, but in the sequel he is supposed to travel in a car. Unless the poet can be charged with having made this blunder, which I think just possible, verse 10 must be considered a later addition.

7. The form of the verb acchahiṃ for acchanti is worthy of note, because hiṃ as ending of the third person plural belongs to Apabhraṃśa. It is interesting to find a true Apabhraṃśa form in a text so old as ours, for it seems to prove that at all times Apabhraṃśa went along with the common Prākṛt, a vulgar or low with a high middle-Indian language.

8. Raivataka is mount Girnār in Kaṭhiawāḍ. The hill is one of the most sacred places of the Jainas, and is covered with temples of the Jinas. It is also sacred to the Hindus on account of its connection with the history of Kṛṣṇa. The poetical description of mount Raivataka forms the subject of the fourth sarga of the Śiśupālavadha by Māgha.

9. The lunar mansion, the chief star of which is Spica or α Virginis.

10. The lamentation of Rājīmatī on her husband's becoming an ascetic forms the subject of a curious Sanskrit poem called Mēmidūtakāvya, by Vikrama, son of Saṅghaṇa, which has been edited in the Kāvyamālā of 1886. It is what is technically called a samasyāpūraṇa or gloss. The last line of each stanza is taken from the Mēghadūta of Kālidāsa, and the first three lines are added by th poet to make the whole fit the circumstances of his tale.

11. Kuccaphaṇaga, in Sanskrit kūrchaphanaka. According to the scholiasts phanaka is a comb made of bamboo.—I have translated, "cut off her tresses," but literally it is: "plucked out her hair." However, I do not think that women also are to pluck out their hair.

12. Rathanēmi was her husband's elder brother. According to a legend told

in Haribhadra's ṭīkā of the Daśavaikālika Sūtra (see Leumann in the Journal of the German Oriental Society, vol. 46, p. 597), Rathanēmi fell in love with Rājīmatī. But that lady in order to make him see his wrong, vomited a sweet beverage she had drunk, in a cup and offered it him. On his turning away with disgust she explained to him her meaning: she too had been vomited, as it were, by Ariṣṭanēmi, notwithstanding which he wanted to have her. She then taught him the Jaina creed, and he became a monk.

13. Suyaṇu = sutanu. This may, however, be a proper name, a synonym of Rājīmatī, for according to the Harivaṃśa 2029 and the Viṣṇu Purāṇa IV, 14, Sutanu was a daughter of Ugrasēna.

14. Vaiśramaṇa is a Prākṛt spelling for Vaiśravaṇa = Kubēra.

15. Nalakūbara is Vaiśramaṇa's son.

16. Indra.

17. The verses 42, 43, 44, 46 have been received in the Daśavaikālika Sūtra II, 7-10, see Leumann's edition of that Sūtra quoted in the note, p. 116. A metrical German translation will be found in the same place.

18. On the Bhōgas see Lecture 15, note 5. It is perhaps here misspelt for Bhōja. In the Viṣṇu Purāṇa, Kaṃsa, Ugrasēna's son, is twice called Bhōjarāja (see Wilson's translation, ed. Hall, vol. iv, pp. 260, 271), in contradiction to the common tradition which makes him an Andhaka, compare Patañjali on Pāṇini IV, 1, 114.

19. There are said to be two kinds of snakes, the gandhana and the agandhana. The former can be made to suck the poison from the wound they have inflicted; the other will rather die than do so. Cf. Leumann, loc. cit., p. 597, note *.

20. Pistia Stratiotes, an aquatic plant.

21. Dēvēndra here refers to the story of the Nūpurapaṇḍita, of which he gives a small portion in Prākṛt. The whole story is related in the Pariśiṣṭaparvan of Hēmachandra, see the introduction to my edition of that work in the Bibliotheca Indica.

22. Compare the last verse of the Ninth Lecture.

Twenty-Third Lecture

1. In this lecture we have a very interesting legend about the way in which the union of the old church of Pārśva and the new church of Mahāvīra was brought about. A revival of this ancient difference seems to have caused the united church afterwards to divide again into the present Śvētāmbara and Digambara sects. They do not continue the two primitive churches, but seem to have grown out of the united church.

2. Pārśva is the last but one Tīrthakara, his Nirvāṇa took place 250 years

before that of Mahāvīra. This statement, which has been generally accepted, is, however, in seeming contradiction to the account of our text, according to which a disciple of Pārśva, who is called a young monk kumāra-śramaṇa, met Gautama, *i.e.* Sudharman, the disciple of Mahāvīra. We therefore must take the word disciple, sīse, as paramparāśiṣya, that is not in its literal sense. See note 8 below.

3. These are the second and third kinds of knowledge according to the Jaina classification. Śruta is the knowledge derived from the sacred books, and avadhi is limited or conditioned knowledge. See Bhandarkar, Report, p. 106.

4. *viz.* the Law of Pārśva or the Law of Mahāvīra.

5. Hence it is called kāujjāma chāturyāma. Chastity (maithunaviramaṇa) was not explicitly enumerated, but it was understood to be contained in the fourth commandment: to have no property (aparigraha).

6. The four kinds of straw are: sālī vīhī koddava rālaga, to which is added hay: raṇṇe taṇāṇi.

7. Bhūya = bhūta, explained Vyantara. The vantara or vānamantara are a class of ghosts. The second part of the word apparently is tara "crossing," and the first seems to contain an accusative vaṃ or vāṇamaṃ which may be connected with viha or vyōman "air."

8. Those under the first Tīrthakaras.

9. The meaning of this explanation is as follows. As the vow of chastity is not explicitly mentioned among Pārśva's four vows, but was understood to be implicityly enjoined by them, it follows that only such men as were of an upright disposition and quick understanding would not go astray by observing the four vows literally, *i.e.* by not abstaining from sexual intercourse, as it was not expressly forbidden.—The argumentation in the text presupposes a decay of the morals of the monastic order to have occurred between Pārśva and Mahāvīra, and this is possible only on the assumption of a sufficient interval of time having elapsed between the last two Tīrthakaras. And this perfectly agrees with the common tradition that Mahāvīra came 250 years after Pārśva.

10. This question does not refer to the difference in doctrines between Pārśva and Mahāvīra, but is discussed here, as the commentator states, for the benefit of the pupils of both sages who are engaged in conversation. I think, however, that this and the following questions are asked and answered here by the disciples of the two Tīrthakaras for a better reason than that given by the scholiast. For in them the leading topics of Jainism are treated in a symbolical way. Gautama at once understands the true meaning of the similes and interprets them to the satisfaction of Kēśi. In this way the unity in doctrine subsisting between the Law of Pārśva and that of Mahāvīra is demonstrated to the hearers of the dispute, after the differences had been explained away.

11. Kaṣāya.

12. In the original "fire" is put in the plural because the four kaṣāyas or cardinal passions are denoted by it.

13. Kanthaka, see Eleventh Lecture, note 2.

14. Māṇasē dukkhē stands for māṇasēhiṃ dukkhēhiṃ. It is an interesting instance of the dropping of case affixes, which probably was more frequent in the vernacular.

Twenty-Fourth Lecture

1. The word I have rendered "article" is māyā, the Sanskrit form of which may be mātā or mātrā. The word is derived from the root mā "to find room in," and denotes that which includes in itself other things, see verse 3. The word may also mean mātri "mother," as Weber understands it. But this is an obviously intentional double meaning.

2. The definitions placed in parentheses in the text are taken from Bhandarkar's Report for 1883-1884, p. 98, note †, p. 100, note *.

3. Ālambana, literally support; explained: supported by which the mind becomes pure.

4. Jāyaṇā = yatna; it consists chiefly in compassion with living creatures (jīvadayā).

5. Upayukta.

6. The "five ways" are vāchanā, etc., as explained in the Twenty-ninth Lecture, §§ 19-23. The commentators supply kuryāt "he should carry on his study."

7. Vikahā = vikathā, which does not occur in common Sanskrit. Perhaps it stands for vikatthā "boasting."

8. Ēṣaṇā.

9. Gavēṣaṇā.

10. Grahaṇaiṣaṇā.

11. Paribhōgaiṣaṇā.

12. There are altogether forty-six faults to be avoided. As they are frequently alluded to in the sacred texts, a systematical enumeration and description of them according to the Dīpikā will be useful.

There are sixteen udgama-dōṣas by which food, etc. becomes unfit for a Jaina monk:

> 1. Ādhākarmika, the fault inherent in food, etc., which a layman has prepared especially for religious mendicants of whatever sect.
>
> 2. Auddēśika, is food, etc., which a layman has prepared for a particular monk.
>
> 3. Pūtika, is food, etc., which is pure on the whole, but contains particles impure on account of the first fault.

4. Unmiśra, is food, etc., of which a part only had been especially prepared for the monk in question.

5. Sthāpanākarmika, is food, etc., which has been reserved for the monk.

6. Prābhṛtika, is food, etc., which has been prepared for some festivity.

7. Prāduḥkaraṇa, when the layman has to light a lamp in order to fetch the alms for the monk.

8. Krīta, when he has to buy the things.

9. Prāmitya, when he has to fetch a ladle (? uddhāraka) in order to draw out the food, etc.

10. Parāvṛtti, when he replaces bad particles of the food by good ones, and vice versa.

11. Adhyāhṛta, when he has to fetch the food, etc., from some distance.

12. Udbhinna, when he has to open locks before he gets at the food, etc.

13. Mālāhṛta, when he has to take the food, etc., from some raised or underground place.

14. Ācchidya, when the food, etc., was taken by force from somebody.

15. Anisṛṣṭa, when a man gives from a store he possesses in common with other men, without asking their permission.

16. Adhyavapūra, when the mendicant calls while the dinner is being cooked, and for his sake more food is put in the pot on the fire. (Some of these faults are enumerated in the Aupapātika Sūtra, § 96, III.)

There are sixteen utpādana-dōṣas; or such faults as are occasioned by the monk's using some means to make the layman give him alms:

1. Dhātrīkarman, when the monk plays with the layman's children.

2. Dūtakarman, when he gives him information about what his people are doing.

3. Nimitta, when he speaks in praise of almsgiving.

4. Ājīvikā, when he makes his birth and family known to him.

5. Vapanīka, when he expatiates upon his misery.

6. Chikitsā, when he cures sick people.

7. Krōdhapiṇḍa, when he extorts alms by threats.

8. Mānapiṇḍa, when he tells the layman that he has laid a wager with other monks that he would get alms from him.

9. Māyāpiṇḍa, when he employs tricks or buffoonery in order to

procure alms.

10. Lōbhapiṇḍa, when he goes begging from a desire of good fare.

11. Saṃstava-piṇḍa, when he flatters the layman.

12. Vidyāpiṇḍa, when he makes a show of his learning; or when he conjures a god from whom to get alms.

13. Mantradōṣa, when he obliges the layman in some way or other.

14. Chūrṇayōga, when he makes himself invisible and then takes away the food, etc.

15. Yōgapiṇḍa, when he teaches people spells, tricks, etc.

16. Mūlakarman, when he teaches them how to obviate evils by roots, charms, etc.

There are ten faults of grahaṇaiṣaṇā:

1. Saṅkita, when a monk accepts alms from a frightened layman.

2. Mrakṣita, when the food is soiled (kharaṇṭita) by animate or inanimate matter.

3. Nikṣipta, when the food is placed among animate things.

4. Pihita, when animate food is covered with inanimate matter, and vice versa.

5. Saṃhṛta, when the layman has to take out the thing to be given from one vessel and puts it into another.

6. Dāyaka, when the condition or occupation of the giver forbids accepting alms from him.

7. Unmiśrita, when the layman mixes up pure with impure food.

8. Aparita (?), when one joint possessor gives away from the store against the other's will.

9. Lipta, when the layman gives food, etc., with a ladle or his hand, soiled with milk, butter, etc.

10. Chardita, when in giving alms he spills milk, etc.

There are four faults of paribhōgaiṣaṇā:

1. Saṃyōjanā, when the monk puts together the ingredients for a good meal.

2. Apramāṇa, when he accepts a greater than the prescribed quantity of food.

3. Iṅgāla, when he praises a rich man for his good fare, or dhūma, when he blames a poor man for his bad fare.

4. Akāraṇa, when he eats choice food on other occasions than those laid down in the sacred texts.

13. Aughika and aupagrahika. The former is explained sāmudāyika, the other denotes such things as are wanted occasionally only, as a stick. I cannot

make out with certainty from the commentaries whether the broom is reckoned among the former or the latter.

14. This means, according to the commentator, either in taking up or putting down, or with respect to the ōgha and aupagrahika outfit, or with respect to substance and condition of mind.

15. This verse, which is in a different metre (āryā), is apparently a later addition, and has probably been taken from an old commentary, the Chūrṇi or the Bhāṣya.

16. Ajjhusirē = asuṣirē, not perforated, not having holes. I translate according tot he author of the Avachūri. The literal translation would give a wrong idea, as it would come to the same as the word bilavarjita in the next verse.

17. *i.e.* where the ground has been cleared not long ago by burning the grass, etc.

18. Ōgāḍhē, where the animate ground is covered by at least five digits of inanimate matter.

19. *viz.* of mind (20, 21), of speech (22, 23), and of the body (24, 25).

20. See Jaina Sutras, Part I: Ākārāṅga Sūtra, Fourth Lecture, Lesson 1, note 2. (*Sacred Books of the East*, vol. 22, p. 150)

21. Saṃrambha.

22. Samārambha.

23. Ārambha.

Twenty-Fifth Lecture

1. Yama etymologically means "restraint"; here it denotes the great vows of the Jainas; cf. Lecture 23:12, and note 5.

2. It is worthy of note that, according to the opinion of our author, the knowledge of astronomy, as taught in the Jyōtiṣa, was one Of the principal accomplishments of a priest. This quality of a priest must therefore have been more conspicuous to an outsider than Brāhmanical books would make us believe.

3. To render muha = mukha.

4. Nakṣatra.

5. Dharma.

6. Jannaṭṭhī vēyasā muham = yajñārthī vedasām mukham. According to the Dīpikā sacrifice here means the ten virtues: truth, penance, content, patience, right conduct, simplicity, faith, constancy, not injuring anything, and Saṃvara.

7. According to the commentators we should translate: He who does not embrace (his people) on meeting them, and is not sorry on leaving them.

8. Niddhantamalapāvagaṃ. The commentator assumes a transposition of the members in this compound. Such irregular compounds are not unfrequent in our Prākṛt. If, however, pāvaga stands for pāpaka, the compound would be regular, and would refer not to "gold," but to the person described. In that case we must translate: whose impurities and sins had been annihilated.

9. *i.e.* by thoughts, words, and acts.

10. Snātaka denotes a Brahman who has finished his studies; it here means as much as "a perfect sage."

11. A various reading in one MS. adds, "Jinas and Brāhmaṇas" before dvijas.

12. Samudāya tayaṃ taṃ tu. The text is evidently corrupted. Samudāya stands, according to the commentators, for samādāya, but there is no finite verb with which to construe the absolute participle, either expressed or easily supplied. Perhaps we must read samuvāya vayaṃ = samuvācha vachas; for the perfect is retained in some cases. However, if this conjecture be right, the next line would be superfluous.

Twenty-Sixth Lecture

1. The southern half of the sky or horizon, between east and west, is divided into four quarters, each of which corresponds in time to a paurușī, the fourth part of a day or a night.

2. A paurușī is the fourth part of a day or a night; about the time of the equinoxes, when the day as well as the night contains twelve hours, the paurușī contains three hours. At the same time, in the months Kaitra and āśvina, as we learn from our verse, the paurușī has three feet, padas. The pada therefore is equal to one hour exactly. The duration of the night at the summer solstice was therefore estimated at eight hours and at the winter solstice at sixteen, just as in the Vedic Jyōtiṣa.

3. A digit, aṅgula, is apparently the twelfth part of a foot, pada = one hour. The digit is therefore equal to five minutes.

4. The fortnights, mentioned in the text, consist of fourteen days only, the remaining ones of fifteen days. In this way the lunar year is made to consist of 354 days.

5. Or thirty, forty, fifty, forty minutes respectively.

6. *i.e.* the nakṣatra which is in opposition to the sun, and accordingly rises at the same time with the setting sun, and sets with the rising sun, compare Rāmāyaṇa III, 16, 12.

7. *i.e.* is about to set.

8. Vērattiya, translated vairātrika; but there is no such word in Sanskrit. It apparently stands for dvairātrika, belonging to two days. As the Hindus reckon the day from sunrise, the time immediately preceding it may be considered to

belong to two days.

9. Compare verse 8.

10. *i.e.* expiation of sins concerning time, cf. Bhandarkar's Report, p. 98, note ‡. It seems to consist in Kāyōtsarga.

11. This is a piece of muslin which the Jaina monks place before their mouth in speaking, in order to prevent insects being drawn in the mouth by the breath.

12. It is here called gōcchaga = gucchaka, originally a bunch of peacocks' feathers, it is so still, if I am not mistaken, with the Digambaras, whilst the Śvētāmbaras use other materials, especially cotton threads.

13. Much in my translation is conjectural. There are some technicalities in these verses which I fail to understand clearly, notwithstanding the explanations of the scholiasts.

14. Vēdikā.

15. I am not sure of having hit the true meaning. The commentators reckon this counting as a fault, while the text itself seems to enjoin it.

16. Dēi paccakkhānaṃ. The meaning is, I believe, that during the time of inspection one should not make up one's mind to abstain from this or that because one is to devote one's whole attention to the inspection of one's things.

17. The Dīpikā places this verse before the last and construes it with verse 29, making out the following meaning: if one, engaged in inspecting his things, converses or gossips, etc., then, being careless in the inspection, he injures, etc.

18. Iriyaṭṭhāē; for one will not be careful about walking (īryā-samiti) if too hungry or thirsty.

19. For one might eat forbidden food if too hungry.

20. It may be remarked here that the verses 25, 16, 19, 20, 24, 26, 27, 29, 33, 34, 35 are in the āryā-metre while the rest of the lecture is in Slōka.

21. Compare note 10 above.

22. Paḍikamittu = pratikramya, explained pratikramaṇasūtram uktvā.

23. According to the Dīpikā: having repeated the three Gāthās beginning āriyauvajjhāya.

24. This verse is the same as verse 18, except a verbal difference in the last line.

25. Paḍikamittu kālassa, see note 10 above. The Dīpikā here explains this phrase by: doing acts proper for that time.

Twenty-Seventh Lecture

1. Gaṇa seems to correspond to the modern Gaccha; see *Sacred Books of the*

East, vol. 22, p. 288, note 2. Gaṇadhara, therefore, does not denote here, as usual, a disciple of Tīrthakara.

2. Khaluṃka = galivṛṣabha. Gali is explained in the dictionaries: a strong but lazy bull. In verse 16 we meet with galigaddaha = galigardabha, as synonymous with khaluṃka.

3. The commentator understands the first line of this verse as having reference to the angry driver. But though an angry driver will perhaps, for all I know, put his bullock's tail to his teeth, still it is harder to supply another subject in the first line than in the second, and in the following verses.

4. Samilā = yugarandhrakīlaka, Avachūri.

5. Chimāla = jāra, see Hēmachandra, Dēśī Kōṣa 3, 27. It is a coarse term, which I replace by another, though probably the language of our coach-drivers might supply us with a more idiomatic rendering.

6. Gārava, cf. Nineteenth Lecture, note 23.

7. The metre of this verse seems to have originally been āryā, but an attempt has been made to change it into Anuṣṭubh. We meet here with the interesting form aṇusāsammī (read aṇusasammi) = anuśāsmi.

8. This seems to be the meaning of the word paliuṃchanti. The commentators say, after other explanations, that they pretend not to have met the person to whom they were sent.

9. Rājaveṭṭhiṃ va mannantā; veṭṭhi = viṣṭi, hire.

Twenty-Eighth Lecture

1. This is usually called mati, and is placed before śruta. The same enumeration recurs in Lecture 33, 4. Umāsvāti in Mōkṣa Sūtra I, 14, gives the following synonyms of mati: smṛti, chintā, abhinibōdha.

2. Maṇanāṇaṃ.

3. Dravya, guṇa, paryāya (pajjava in Jaina Prākṛt). Guṇa, quality, is generally not admitted by the Jainas as a separate category, see Śīlāṅka's refutation of the Vaiśēṣika doctrines at the end of his comments on Sūtrakṛtāṅga I, 12 (Bombay edition, p. 482).

4. They are frequently called astikāyas, or realities.

5. It is here called nabhas instead of ākāśa.

6. Avagāha.

7. Vartanā.

8. Upayōga.

9. Singleness (ēkatva) makes a thing appear as one thing, separateness (pṛthaktva) as different from others.

10. Sahasamuiya = svayaṃsamudita. It is usually rendered sahasammati.

11. Āsravasaṃvara, see above, verse 14, 6 and 7.

12. A chadmastha is one who has not yet obtained Kēvala, or the highest knowledge; he is in the two guṇasthānas (the fourteen stages in the development of the soul from the lowest to the highest) characterised as 1. upaśāntamōha, and 2. kṣīṇamōha; *viz.* 1. that in which delusion is only temporarily separated from the soul, and 2. that in which delusion is finally destroyed.

13. Bāhira; apparently the same works are intended which are elsewhere called anaṅgapraviṣṭa.

14. The original has the singular.

15. The seven nayas are "points of view or principles with reference to which certain judgments are arrived at or arrangements made." Bhandarkar, Report, p. 112.

16. Pravachana.

17. *e.g.* that of Kapila, etc., Comm.

18. Dharma.

19. Astikāya; see note on verse 7.

20. *i.e.* true things as soul, etc.

21. Saṃyaktva "righteousness."

22. Charaṇaguṇa. The commentators make this a dvandva compound, and interpret charaṇa as vratādi, and guṇa as piṇḍaviśuddhi, etc.

23. By deliverance I have rendered mōkṣa, and by final perfection nirvāṇa. Mōkṣa denotes freedom from Karman, a condition which in Brāhmanical philosophy is called jīvanmukti.

24. Nivvitigicchā = nirvichikitsa. According to the commentary it may stand for nir-vid-jugupsā "without loathing the saints."

25. See Bhandarkar, Report, p. 98, note ‡.

26. The Dīpikā contains the following details. Nine monks resolve to live together for eighteen months. They make one of their number their superior, kalpasthita, four become parihārikas, and the remaining four serve them (anuparihārikas). After six months the parihārikas become anuparihārikas and vice versa. After another six months the kalpasthita does penance and all the other monks serve him as anuparihārikas.

Twenty-Ninth Lecture

1. Here we have no less than ten verbs, many of which are synonyms, with probably no well-defined difference in their meaning. This heaping of synonymous words is a peculiarity of the archaic style. The commentators always labour hard to assign to each word an appropriate meaning, but by sometimes offering different sets of explanations they show that their ingenuity of interpretation was not backed by tradition.

2. Or aversion to the Circle of Births.

3. In this way all paragraphs up to § 72 open with a question of always the same form. I drop the question in the sequel.

4. Atyāśātana.

5. Nidāna, cf. Thirteenth Lecture, note 5.

6. This is the meaning of the words itthīvēya napuṃsagavētaṃ = strīvēda, napuṃsakavēda, as explained by the commentators on Lecture Thirty-Two, 102.

7. Karaṇaguṇaśrēdhīm pratipadyatē. It is difficult to render this phrase adequately; the meaning is that by successively destroying moral impurities one arrives at higher and higher virtues.

8. Yōga, *i.e.* the cause of the production of Karman.

9. Ghāti, compare Bhandarkar, Report, p. 93, note *.

10. See Twenty-fourth Lecture, note 1.

11. Expiatory rites, ālōchanā, etc.

12. Antakriyā, explained by mukti.

13. The Kalpas and the Vimānas are the heavens of the Vaimānika gods, see Thirty-Sixth Lecture, verse 208 etc.

14. By road is meant the means of acquiring right knowledge, and by the reward of the road, right knowledge. The reward of good conduct is mukti.

15. Savvapāṇabhūyajīvasattā. The prāṇas possess from two to four organs of sense, the jīvas five, the bhūtas are plants, and the sattvas are all remaining beings.

16. According to the commentaries, by Tīrtha are meant the Gaṇadharas.

17. Concerning the eight kinds of Karman, see Thirty-third Lecture, verses 2 and 3. āyuṣka is that Karman which determines the length of time which one is to live. A somewhat different explanation of this Karman is given by Bhandarkar, loc. cit., p. 97, note.

18. The passage in question is an addition in some MSS., as the commentators tell us. The meaning seems to be that the Karman which was attached to many parts of the soul is restricted to fewer places by the influence of the purity superinduced on the soul by pondering.

19. Vyavadāna is the cutting off of the Karman and the subsequent purity of the soul.

20. Sambhōga = ēkamaṇḍalyām āhārakaraṇam.

21. Ālambanā, glānatādi.

22. Duccaṃ suhase.gjaṃ uvasaṃpajjittāṇaṃ viharai.

23. Except such as are obligatory, *e.g.* his broom, the mukhavastrikā, etc.

24. Samāhiē = samāhita or samādhimān.

25. Sadbhāva pratyākhyāna. The Dīpikā gives the following explanation: he

makes the renunciation in such a way that he need not make it a second time.

26. Vēdanīya is that Karman which produces effects that must be experienced, as pleasure or pain; āyuṣka is the Karman that determines the length of life; nāman and gōtra cause him to be born as such or such an individual in this or that family; see Thirty-third Lecture, verses 2 and 3.

27. Explained: sthavirakalpasādhuvēṣadhāritvam.

28. Appaḍilēha = alpapratyupēkṣa; he has to inspect few things, because he uses only few.

29. Gupti.

30. For Saṃvara and āsrava, see above, Twelfth Lecture, note 8, and Sixteenth Lecture, note 2.

31. See above, § 41.

32. Here is a pun on the word sutta = sūtra, which means thread and Sūtra, sacred lore, or knowledge acquired by the study of the Sūtras.

33. *i.e.* makes it contain nothing foreign to its own nature.

34. Sēlēsī = śailēśī; śailēśa is Mēru, and its avasthā, or condition, is śailēśī.

35. Or, perhaps, which results in experiencing anger.

36. There are sixteen kaṣāyas, nine nō-kaṣāyas, and three mōhanīyas.

37. These are the obstacles to the five kinds of knowledge: mati, śruta, avadhi, manaḥparyāya, kēvala.

38. They are: the obstacles to chakṣurdarśana, to achakṣurdarśana, to avadhidarśana, and to kēvaladarśana, and five kinds of sleep (nidrā). Concerning Antarāya, see Thirty-third Lecture, verses 2-3.

39. Sayōgin, *i.e.* while he has not yet reached the fourteenth guṇasthāna, the state of a Kēvalin.

40. Airyapathika.

41. *i.e.* when he has become a Kēvalin, as described in the preceding paragraph.

42. Sukladhyāna.

43. See note on § 41.

Thirtieth Lecture

1. Karmōpādānahētavas, that through which the soul becomes affected by Karman.

2. Agārava = agaurava; but it is here explained, free from garva, cf. Nineteenth Lecture, note 23.

3. Literally krores, *i.e.* ten millions.

4. Comp. Aupapātika Sūtra, ed. Leumann, p. 38 ff. The general division is the same, but the subdivision differs in many details.

5. Gradual reduction of food, from a full meal of thirty-two morsels to one

of one morsel.

6. Angōpāṅgādikam saṃvṛtya pravartanam, Ṭīkā.

7. The meaning of this singular statement is as follows. If four fasts of two, three, four, and five days are performed in this order, they form a line. If this set of fasts is four times repeated, each time beginning with a different number, we get sixteen fasts; they form a square, *viz.*:

1 . 2 . 3 . 4
2 . 3 . 4 . 1
3 . 4 . 1 . 2
4 . 1 . 2 . 3

The next class contains 64 fasts, the fourth 4,096, the fifth 16,777,216 fasts. Fasts of the last class require 700,000 years at least, and must be assumed to be restricted to former Tīrthakaras, whose lives lasted enormous periods of time.

8. Saparikarma = vaiyāvṛtyasahita. This leads to iṅginīmaraṇa and bhaktapratyakhyāna; the aparikarma to pādapōpagamana (*i.e.* prāyōpagamana); comp. *Sacred Books of the East*, vol. 22, p. 72.

9. Thirty-two mouthfuls is the usual quantity of food of men, twenty-eight that of women. A mouthful is of the size of an egg.

10. Nagara, where no taxes (na kara) are levied, while villages pay eighteen taxes.

11. Nigama, or a place where many merchants dwell.

12. Pallī.

13. Khēṭa.

14. Karvaṭa. According to the dictionary, it means "market-town"; but the commentators render it by kunagara, or say that it is karvaṭajanāvāsa, the dwelling-place of the Karvaṭa people.

15. Drōṇamukha, a town to which there is access by water and land, like Bhṛgukaccha or Tāmralipti.

16. Paṭṭana.

17. Maṭamba, a town which is more than three and a half yōjanas distant from the next village.

18. Sambādha, prabhūtachāturvarṇyanivāsa.

19. A dwelling-place of Bhikṣus, or a dēvagṛha.

20. Sannivēśa.

21. Samāja.

22. These are terms for different kinds of collecting alms; it is called pēṭā (box), when one begs successively at four houses forming the corners of an imaginary square; gōmūtrikā, when he takes the houses in a zigzag line; pataṅgavīthikā (cricket's walk), when he goes to houses at a great distance

from one another; śambūkāvartta (the windings of a conch), when he goes in a spiral line, either toward the centre (abhyantara) or from the centre outward (bahis); āyataṃ-gatvā-pratyāgata, when he first goes straight on and then returns.

23. I give the traditional explanation of the verses, as handed down in the commentaries. If we might set it aside, I should translate: abstinence with reference to disposition is observed by him who in collecting alms preserves the same disposition, whether he has to do with a woman or man, etc.

24. For development (pajjava = paryāya) denotes any form or phase of existence which anything can assume. Therefore all particulars of place, *e.g.* are developments of Place. As all restrictions of place, etc., indirectly diminish the food obtainable by a monk, they also come under the head Abstinence.

25. According to the commentator, these are the six kinds enumerated in verse 29. Sambūkāvartta is of two kinds, as explained in the note; the eighth kind is ṛjvī, or the common way of begging. These eight ways have reference to the houses in which they collect alms. The seven ēṣaṇās refer to the quality or quantity of the food; their names are given in the ṭīkā, partly in Prākṛt, partly in Sanskrit: 1. saṃsaṭṭhā; 2. asaṃsaṭṭhā; 3. uddhaḍā; 4. alpalēpikā; 5. udgṛhītā; 6. pragṛhītā; 7. ujjhitadharmā. According to another passage: 1. is saṃspṛṣṭa, 3. uddhrita, 5. avagṛhīta.

26. Praṇīta, explained puṣṭikara.

27. Viōsagga, viussaga, viusagga. It is usually rendered vyutsarga, but the Sanskrit prototype is vyavasarga, as Leumann has pointed out, l.c., p. 152.

28. Compare Aupapātika Sūtra, ed. Leumann, p. 40.

29. Ibidem, p. 42.

30. They are enumerated in the following Gāthā: āyariya-uvajjhāē thēra-tavassī-gilāṇa-sēhāṇa | sāhhmmiya-kula-gaṇa-saṅgha-saṃgayaṃ tam iha kāyavvaṃ. The ten persons or body of persons entitled to "service" are: 1. āchārya; 2. upādhyāya; 3. sthavira; 4. tapasvin; 5. glāna; 6. śaikṣa; 7. sādharmika; 8. kula; 9. gaṇa; 10. saṅgha.

31. This is the ārtaraudradhyāna.

Thirty-First Lecture

1. This lecture offers many difficulties to the translator, as it contains scarcely more than a dry list of articles of the Jaina faith. To fully understand or interpret it would require an accurate knowledge of the complete religious system of the Jainas, to which we can lay no claim at present. The order in which the articles are given follows the number of their subdivisions. In some cases the number is not given in the Sūtra, but is supplied by the commentary.

2. Compare Lecture Nineteen, 91, and Thirty, 3. Hurtful acts (daṇḍa) are

threefold, as referring to thoughts, words, and acts; conceited acts (gārava), as pride of riches, of taste (rasa), and of pleasure or fashion (sātā); delusive acts (śalya), as māyā, nidāna, and mithyādarśana.

3. Vikatthā.

4. Saṃjñā.

5. Yatatē "exerts himself"; supply "to avoid, to know, or to do," as the case may require.

6. Kriyā; they are: 1. kāyikī; 2. adhikaraṇikī; 3. prādvēṣikī; 4. paritāpanikī, and 5. prāṇātipātikī.

7. On the lēśyās see Thirty-fourth Lecture, note 1.

8. From the commentaries I learn two more of these six kāraṇas: vēdana and vaiyāvṛtya. I cannot say which are the remaining three.

9. They are enumerated in the Thirtieth Lecture, note 25.

10. *viz.* caste, family, beauty, etc.; see Sūtrakṛt. II, 2, 17.

11. Brahmagupti. This is of nine kinds.

12. Bhikṣudharma. It consists of Nos. 46-49, 26, 27, of Lecture Twenty-Nine, truth, purity, poverty, and chastity.

13. The details given in the commentary (Dēvēndra) partly differ from the description of the twelve duties of Śrāvakas, and the ten duties of Bhikṣus given by Bhandarkar from the Kārttikēyānuprēkṣā, see his Report, p. 114 ff.

14. Paramādhārmika. My translation is based on the enumeration of fifteen words, among which the names of some well-known hells occur.

15. The sixteen lectures of the first part of the Sūtrakṛtāṅga, the last of which is called Gāthā, are meant by the sixteen Gāthās. The whole book contains twenty-three lectures as stated in verse 16.

16. The first śrutaskandha of the Jñātādharmakathā, which contains nineteen adhyayanas, is intended by jñātādhyayana.

17. Śabala, because they "variegate" the conduct. The actions meant are sitting on an unwiped seat, etc.

18. Parīsaha, see above, Second Lecture.

19. Rūpa. The twenty-four gods are: ten Bhavanapatis, eight Vyantaras, five Jyōtiṣkas, one Vaimānika; or the 24 prophets.

20. Bhāvanā, the subdivisions of the five great vows, see *Sacred Books of the East*, vol. 22, p. 189 ff.

21. The Daśāśrutaskandha, Bṛhat Kalpa, and Vyavahāra Sūtras are meant, which together contain twenty-six uddēśas.

22. *i.e.* the Āchārāṅga Sūtra; it now contains but twenty-four lectures, but is said to have originally contained four more, see *Sacred Books of the East*, vol. 22, introduction, p. xlix f. These four lectures were: Mahāparinnā, Ugghāya, Aṇugghāya, Ārōvaṇā.

23. The pure operations of mind, speech, and body.

24. As far as I can make out from the enumeration in the commentary, they are articles regulating the intercourse between monks, especially pupils and teacher.

Thirty-Second Lecture

1. By beginningless time the Saṃsāra is meant; its causes are the kaṣāyas or cardinal passions, and avirati.

2. Saccassa = satyasya. This is a various reading; the received text has savvassa. The commentators give the following explanation: by the property of knowledge to make everything known—this indicates that knowledge is the cause of mōkṣa.

3. Samādhi; the Dīpikā explains it by jñānadarśanachāritralābha.

4. Balāka.

5. Tṛṣṇā.

6. Rasā.

7. Dṛptikara.

8. Duttara.

9. Suuttara.

10. Trichosanthes Palmata, or Cucumis Colocynthus.

11. Compare verse 4.

12. Love and Hatred must of course be understood in their widest meaning. The same remark applies to the term "colour," which according to Hindu terminology denotes everything that is perceived by the eye. The first three sentences are, in the original, dependent on verbs as vadanti, āhus. I have, here and elsewhere, dropped them in the translation.

13. Rūvāṇugāsāṇuga = rūpa-anuga-āśā-anuga. This division of the compound looks artificial; I should prefer to divide rūva-aṇugāsa-aṇuga = rūpa-anukarṣa-anuga; literally, possessed of attraction by colours.

14. Rūvaṇuvāēṇa pariggahēṇa. Parigraha is explained as the desire to possess them.

15. Instead of "lying," we can also adopt the rendering "stealing," as the word in the original mōsa may stand either for mṛṣā, or for mōṣa.

16. Aṇissa = aniśra. Niśrā does not occur in common Sanskrit; it is rendered avaṣṭambha by the commentators.

17. Arati and rati. Compare note on Lecture Twenty-One, 21, where I have adopted another translation suited to the context. The first four numbers contain the cardinal passions; the rest the emotions which are called nō-kaṣāya.

18. My translation follows the interpretation of the commentators. The

original runs thus: Kappaṃ na icchijja sahāyalicchū pacchāṇutāvēṇa tavappabhāvaṃ. The meaning they have made out is very unsatisfactory. There is a remarkable various reading in MS. C not noticed by the scholiasts: sahāyalacchiṃ = svabhāvalakṣmīṃ. If this was the original reading, the meaning of the line, in which however I must leave the word kappam untranslated, would come to this: a monk who regrets having taken the vows should not desire personal power as the reward for his penance. Kalpa, according to the commentators, is one who is able to perform his religious duties; a kalpa is contrasted with a śiṣya, novice.

19. Saṃkalpavikalpanāsu upasthitasya.

Thirty-Third Lecture

1. Compare Bhandarkar, Report, p. 93, note *.

2. Nos. 1-4 are nidrā, prachalā, nidrānidrā, prachalāprachalā; I render the etymological meaning of these words. According to the Dīpikā, however, they have a different meaning: nidrā means the state of agreeable waking; prachalā, the slumber of a standing or sitting person; nidrānidrā, deep sleep; prachalāprachalā, sleep of a person in motion. Nos. 6 and 7 are here called chakkhu and achakkhu, instead of ābhinibōdhika and śruta.

3. The divisions of the second Karman are the feelings or emotions enumerated in the 102nd verse of the last lecture, from disgust onward. There are seven of them, if desire for women, men, or both, is reckoned as one item, but nine, if it is reckoned as three. The sixteen divisions of the Karman produced by the cardinal passions are arrived at by subdividing each of the four passions with reference to 1. anantānubandha; 2. pratyākhyāna; 3. apratyākhyāna; 4. saṃjvalana.

4. In the Dīpikā 103 subdivisions are enumerated; they correspond to our genera.

5. 3. Bhōga, 4. upabhōga; bhōga is enjoyment of flowers, food, etc.; upabhōga, that of ones house, wife, etc. The Karman in question brings about an obstruction to the enjoyment, etc., though all other circumstances be favourable.

6. The Karman is considered to consist, like other substances, of atoms, here called pradēśa point. The word I have translated number of atoms is paēsaggaṃ = pradēsāgram, which is rendered paramāṇuparimāṇa.

7. Gaṇṭhiyasatta = granthigasattva.

8. The six directions of space are the four cardinal points, zenith and nadir. The commentators quote scripture that ēkēndriyas, or beings with one organ of sense, are bound by Karman in three and more directions. The true meaning of this statement is beyond my grasp.—The Dīpikā explains how

Karman acts on the soul. The soul absorbs all material particles of a suitable nature (especially the karmapudgalas) with which it comes into contact, *i.e.* all that are in the same space with the soul, and assimilates them in the form of jñānāvaranīya, etc., just as fire consumes everything within its reach, but nothing beyond it.

9. *i.e.* 3,000,000,000,000,000 Sāgarōpamās.

10. Anubhāga, explained karmarasaviśēṣa.

Thirty-Fourth Lecture

1. The lēśyās (adhyavasāya viśēṣāḥ) are different conditions produced in the soul by the influence of different Karman; they are therefore not dependent on the nature of the soul, but on the Karman which accompanies the soul, and are, as it were, the reflection of the Karman on the soul, as stated in the following verse from the Avachūri:

kṛṣṇādidravyasāchivyāt pariṇāmō ya ātmanaḥ |
spaṭikasyēva tatrāyaṃ lēśyāśabdaḥ pravartate ||

The alteration produced on the soul, just as on a crystal by the presence of black things, etc., is denoted by the word lēśyā. The Lēśyā, or, according to the above explanation, what produces Lēśyā, is a subtile substance accompanying the soul; to it are attributed the qualities described in this lecture.—The word lēsā is derived from klēśa; this etymology appears rather fanciful, but I think it may be right. For the Lēśyās seem to be the Klēśas, which affect the soul, conceived as a kind of substance. The Sanskrit term Lēśyā is of course a hybrid word. It must, however, be stated that lēsā occurs also in the meaning "colour," *e.g.* Sūtrakṛt. I, 6, 13, and that the Prākṛt of klēsa is kilēśa.

2. Sapindus Detergens.

3. It is not the common Aśōka, Jonesia Asoka, which has red flowers.

4. Corarias Indica, blue jay; according to some, a kingfisher.

5. Linum Usitatissimum, whose flowers are blue.—The word for grey is kāū = kāpōta; in the comm., however, it is described as kiṃchit kṛṣṇā, kiṃchil lōhitā, which would be rather brown. But the description given in our verse leaves no doubt that grey colour is intended.

6. Crotolaria Juncea.

7. Terminalia Tomentosa.

8. Aṅka, maṇiviśēṣa.

9. Jasminum Multiflorum.

10. The gourd Lagenaria Vulgaris.

11. Azadirachta Indica.

12. The aggregate of three spices, etc., black and long pepper and dry ginger.

13. Feronia Elephantum.

14. A kind of intoxicating drink, extracted from the blossoms of Lythrum Fructicosum, with sugar, etc.

15. Acacia Sirisa.

16. The Lēśyās may possess their qualities in a low, middle, or high degree; each of these degrees is again threefold, *viz.* low, middle, and high. In this way the subdivision is carried on up to 243.

17. *i.e.* commits the five great sins.—The following verses give the character —lakṣaṇa—of the Lēśyās.

18. This is, according to the comm., the meaning of the word niddhaṃdhasapariṇāmō.

19. Paliuñchaga-uvahiya = pratikuñchaka-upadhika.

20. Yōgavān upaḍhānavān.

21. Literally: who avoids the ārta and raudra dhyānas, and practises the dharma and śukla dhyānas. These terms cannot be adequately translated; the reader may therefore be referred for details to Bhandarkars Report, p. 110 ff.

22. Ṭhāṇāiṃ sthānāni.

23. Samaya is the smallest division of time = instant, moment.

24. *viz.* as denizens of hell, brutes, men, and gods. Only the three first Lēśyās lead to being born in hell.

25. The consequence of this statement appears to be that at the expiration of the Lēśyā a new one is produced. The commentators, however, are not explicit on this head.

26. About the former years, see above, Third Lecture, note 2.

27. This verse seems to lay down the duration of the Lēśyā in the case of common gods, while the next one applies to Bhavanapatis, etc.

28. The question treated rather darkly in the next three verses is, according to the comm., the following:—Every individual dies in the same Lēśyā in which he is born. When his Lēśyā ends with his life, then the soul must get a new Lēśyā. Our verses state at which time the new Lēśyā comes into existence or is joined with the soul.

Thirty-Fifth Lecture

1. Buddhēhi.

2. Ullōva = ullōcha.

3. Parakaḍa = parakṛta, explained parair ātmārthaṃ kṛta.

4. Śukla dhyāna, see Thirty-Fourth Lecture, note 21.

5. By the destruction of the vīryāntarāya.

Thirty-Sixth Lecture

1. It will perhaps not be amiss to give a systematic list of the subjects treated in this lecture. The numbers refer to the verses.

A. Things without life, 3-48
  (1) Without form, 5-9
  (2) With form, 10-48
B. Living Beings, 48-246
  (1) Perfected souls, 50-68
  (2) Mundane Beings, 69-246
    a. Immovable Beings, 71-106
      α. Earth Lives, 71-84
      β. Water Lives, 85-92
      γ. Plants, 93-106
    b. Movable Beings, 108-246
      α. Fire Lives, 109-117
      β. Wind Lives, 118-126
      γ. Beings with an organic body, 127-246
        i. With two organs of sense, 128-136
        ii. With three organds of sense, 137-145
        iii. With four organs of sense, 146-155
        iv. With five organs of sense, 156-246
          a. Denizens of hell, 157-170
          b. Animals (vertebratae), 171-193
            1. Aquatic, 171-178
            2. Terrestrial, 179-186
            3. Aerial, 187-193
          c. Men, 194-202
          d. Gods, 203-246
            1. Bhavanavāsin, 205, 218
            2. Vyantara, 206, 219
            3. Jyōtiṣka, 207, 220
            4. Vaimānika, 208, 221-246
              a'. Living in Kalpas, 209, 210, 221-232
              b'. Living above the Kalpas, 211
                α'. Graivēyakas, 212, 213, 233-241
                β'. Anuttaras, 214-217, 242, 243

Appendix, 247-267.

2. Jīva and ajīva. The former is defined in the Dīpikā as upayōgavān in accordance with our text, Lecture Twenty-Eight, 10; the latter is also called pudgala.

3. It is here called addhā-samaya, which may be translated real-time. It has no divisions or parts as the other things, because of time only the present moment is existent. And a moment cannot be divided.

4. Time is only present in the two and a half continents inhabited by men, and the oceans belonging to them; beyond this sphere there is no time or, as the Dīpikā correctly remarks, no divisions of time.

5. Saṃtatiṃ pappa = saṃtatim prāpya.

6. According to the Dīpikā, we should have but two divisions, *viz.*: 1. compound things (skandha, aggregates of atoms), and 2. not aggregated atoms; for Nos. 2 and 3 of our text are but subdivisions of No. 1.

7. Ēgattēṇa puhuttēṇa = katvēna pṛthaktvēna.

8. The meaning of this verse is that a thing, as far as its material cause is concerned, has always existed, and will ever exist under one form or other, but that the individual thing in its present form has but a limited existence.

9. Asaṃkhakālam. See Tenth Lecure, note 3.

10. Antaram; the interval between the thing being removed from its proper scene and reaching it again (Avachūri and Dīpikā).

11. Each verse has the same form as 23, only that another colour is substituted for black. In the same way the subdivisions of smells, etc., are given. I give the first verse of each class and abbreviate the rest.

12. The greatest size (ōgāhaṇā) of men is 500 dhanus, or 2,000 cubits, the smallest one cubit.

13. Similar details are given in the Aupapātika Sūtra (ed. Leumann, § 163 f.).

14. According to the commentator, who quotes scripture, it decreases an aṅgula every Yōjana.

15. Compare Lecture Thirty-Four, 9 and note. The commentators here treat aṅka as a separate substance without offering any explanation. The Dīpikā writes sītā instead of śītā.

16. Or 333⅓dhanus.

17. The words translated, "considered singly" and "considered collectively," are ēgattēṇa and puhuttēṇa = ēkatvēna and pṛthaktvēna. Their usual meaning has been given in verse 11.

18. Lavaṇāsē?

19. Not in our dictionaries; the commentators only say that it is a kind of mineral, dhātuviśēṣa. I give the Sanskrit names of the stones, which cannot be identifies with certainty, or are not contained in the index of R. Garbe's work on the Indian minerals, Leipzig, 1882.

20. A medicinal earth, commonly called Kaṅkuṣṭha.

21. The enumeration contains thirty-nine, instead of thirty-six items, as stated in verses 73 and 76.

22. The meaning seems to be that souls of earth-bodies live in earth-bodies, the time stated in verse 82, while the length of each separate existence is determines in verse 81.

23. Guccha; it is explained to denote such plants from the single root or bulb of which come forth many stalks, *e.g.* Vṛntāka, Solanum Melongena.

24. Gulma, similar to the preceding class, but bringing forth twigs or stems, instead of stalks, *e.g.* Navamālikā, Jasminum Sambac, Kaṇavīra, etc.

25. Latā, as Lotus, Pandanus, etc.

26. Vallī, as gourds, Piper Betel, etc.

27. Tṛṇa, grass. But of the two examples given in the commentary, juñjuka is not in our dictionaries, and Arjuna denotes usually a tree, Terminalia Arjuna.

28. Valaya; so called from their foliation.

29. Parvaga, as sugar-cane.

30. Kuhaṇa, plants which cause the earth to burst, as sarpacchatra, mushroom (toad-stool).

31. Ōṣadhi, such plants as die after having brought forth seed, as rice, etc.

32. Haritakāya, as taṇḍulēya, etc.

33. The plants in the following list are, according to the commentary, mostly bulbs, "well known in the countries where they grow." Many of them are not in our dictionaries. I give the Prākṛt form of their names, and note the Sanskrit equivalent when it can be identified.

34. Āluka, Amorphophallus Campanulatus.

35. Mūlaka, radish.

36. A various reading has for the last two words (which might be differently divided), ā paikkēikandalī. The Kandalī, the plantain-tree, occurs in the next line again.

37. A various reading is Kuḍambaya.

38. Kṛṣṇakanda, Nymphaea Rubra.

39. Vajrakanda of the Sanskrit Koṣas.

40. Śūraṇa, Arum Campanulatum.

41. Aśvakarṇā. Aśvakarṇa is a tree, Vatika Robusta.

42. Utkalikā, intermittent winds.

43. Maṇḍalikā = vātōlī.

44. According to the comm. these winds blow on the oceans which are situated below the Ratnaprabhā-hell, or which support the heavenly Vimānas, and have the density of snow. Perhaps the notion is similar to that of the Hindu astronomers, who fancied that the heavenly bodies were set in motion by cords of wind called pravaha. See Sūrya Siddhānta II, 3.

45. This seems to be the hurricane which causes the periodical destruction

of the world. But Dēvēndra says: "Saṃvartaka is a wind which carries grass, etc., from the outside into a particular place."

46. Though in the preceding verse it was said that there are five kinds of wind, six are enumerated, and more are implied by the etc.

47. As many of these lower animals are not known to us, I give the Prākṛt names of those which I cannot identify. Dēvēndra says: "Some of them are well known, the remaining ones are to be explained according to tradition." The explanation of this passage in the Avachūri is fuller.

48. A small poisonous animal. Petersburg Dictionary, s. v. According to the Jīvavichāra Vṛtti V, 16, they are earth-snakes (bhūnāga), which originate in the rainy season when the sun is in Aśleṣā, *i.e.* about the beginning of July.

49. Mātṛvāhaka. According to the description of the Avachūri, the larvae of Phryganeae seem intended. According to the Jīvavichāra Vṛtti, they are called chūḍēlī in Guzeratī.

50. Vāsīmukha, explained: Whose mouth is like a chisel or adze. There are many insects, *e.g.* the Curculionidae, which suit this description.

51. Śaṅkhānaka, very small, conch-like animals.

52. Chandaṇa = Akāvṛkṣa (?). According to the Jīvavichāra Vṛtti V, 16, they are animals living in water and on land, and are called Akṣa in the vernacular (samayabhāṣā).

53. Kunthu or animalcules are also called Aṇuddharī, see concerning them, Kalpa Sūtra, Rules for Yatis, § 44, *Sacred Books of the East*, vol. 22, p. 304.—I give in the text the Prākṛt form of the words I cannot identify.

54. Mālūka is the name of a plant, Ocimum Sanctum. It must, of course, here denote some animal.—The Jīvavichāra enumerates many other animals, lice, bugs, different kinds of larvae living in dung, corn, etc.—The tṛṇahāra, kāṣṭhahāra, and patrahāra seem to denote different kinds of ants.

55. Kukkuṭa is given in the dictionaries as the name of a small lizard.

56. Nandyāvarta occurs elsewhere as the name of a particular fish, and of a shell. It can be neither of these in our passage, as both animals belong to other classes than the Chaturindriyas.

57. Etymologically: with many-coloured wings. Probably butterflies are intended.

58. Tirikkha = tiryak. Apparently only the higher animals are intended by this term, the lower animals, from the insects downwards, being enumerated in the preceding classes of beings.

59. It will be seen that the longest duration of life in each hell is always equal to the shortest in the preceding one.

60. Sammūrchima. They grow by assimilating the materials in their surrounding. According to a second explanation, their internal organ does not

fully develop.

61. See Third Lecture, note 2.

62. This is, according to the Avachūri, the meaning of puhuttaṃ pṛthaktvam.

63. *e.g.* the charmachaṭakas or bats.

64. Samudga. These interesting birds are said to live outside the Mānuṣōttara, or world inhabited by men.

65. The comm. do not tell us what kind of birds is intended.

66. The comm. do not explain this expression; the meaning, therefore, is doubtful. I give a literal translation of it in this and the next. verse.

67. See above, note 60, on verse 171.

68. Concerning Karmabhūmi, see part i, p.195, note 1. The Avachūri places the Akarmabhūmi first, but the next verse proves that it originally stood in the second place.

69. These are seven groups of islands situated off the eastern and western ends of the Himālaya, which are inhabited by fabulous races.

70. According to the Avachūri, there are five kinds in Bharata, five in Airāvata, and five in Vidēha.

71. *viz.* five in each of the six Akarmabhūmis: Haimavata, Harivarṣa, Hairaṇyavata, Dēvakuru, and Uttarakuru.

72. According to the commentaries the word kumāra is to be supplied after each of the ten names.

73. They are termed Kalpōpaga and Kalpātīta.

74. I am not sure that these are the correct Sanskrit forms of the two last Kalpas; the original has āṇaya and Pāṇaya.

75. *i.e.* those who live on the neck (grīva), *i.e.* on the upper part of the universe.

76. *i.e.* those above whom there dwell no other gods.

77. From this verse to verse 241 the length of life increases by one Sāgarōpamā in each following class of gods.

78. *viz.* Vijaya, Vaijayanta, Jayanta, and Aparājita.

79. Two MSS. (A and D) insert after verses 245 the following two verses: The longest interval between a Graivēyika's leaving his rank in ānata, etc., and being again born to it, is an endless time, the shortest is from two to nine years. In the case of Anuttara gods the longest interval is a Sāgarōpamā plus one Saṃkhyēya, the shortest is from two to nine years.

80. Naya.

81. The last self-mortification, saṃlekhanā, which is to end with death, is intended here. Some details about it will be found in *Sacred Books of the East*, vol. 22, p. 74 ff.

82. Vigaī-nijjūhaṇa. The meaning is that at the end of his fasts a monk should eat āchāmla, nirvikṛtika, etc. In the Avachūri a verse from the Niśīthachūrni is quoted, which gives the same rule for the second four years.

83. Āyāma = āchāmla. Is this the same thing as the āyāmaga = āchāmaka mentioned in Lecture Fifteen, 13? See Fifteenth Lecture, note 7.

84. Kōḍīsahiyam āyamam = kōṭisahitam āchāmlam. The commentators give two explanations of this phrase: (1) Having fasted one day, one should take āchāmla on the next day; (2) one should on the second day continue to abstain from āchāmla.

85. The definition of these technical terms is given below, verses 262 ff.

86. Ālōkanā = śramaṇaphalam. The Avachūri renders the last phrase: "They are able to bring about the salvation of others." The original, however, has sōuṃ, "to hear."

87. The Abhiyōgidēvas are genii who serve the gods. This Bhāvanā leads to being born as an Abhiyōgidēva; the next two Bhāvanās, as a Kilviṣadēva and an Asura.

88. Uttarajjhāē in the original. The commentators give uttara here the meaning pradhāna, "best, prominent." The same explanation is given by the scholiast on the Nandī (Weber, Sacred Literature of the Jains, p.124). Perhaps the name refers to the tradition that Mahāvīra recited at the time of his death the thirty-six apuṭṭha-vāgaraṇāiṃ, which are identified by one commentator of the Kalpa Sūtra (Lives of the Jinas, § 147) with the Uttarādhyayana; for uttara also means "last."

89. Bhavasiddhīya = bhavasiddhika, explained by bhavya.

CPSIA information can be obtained
at www.ICGtesting.com
Printed in the USA
FSHW020524140120
66073FS

9 781515 192145